The
CHICKtionary

Praise for Anna Lefler and *The Chicktionary*

"I have to tell you that Anna Lefler's *The Chicktionary* is pure genius. I always knew she was funny but the definitions you will find in this must-read guide to the way women speak are sure to make you laugh until you pee."

~ Stefanie Wilder-Taylor, comedian and author of *Sippy Cups Are Not for Chardonnay: And Other Things I Had to Learn as a New Mom*

"Anna Lefler is an American original. She isn't merely blazingly smart and achingly funny. She's also so utterly *sympatico* with what women think and how women talk that years from now sociologists will be consulting *The Chicktionary* as the only true and tested source on the challenging but wholly worthy subject. The English language has a true friend in Anna. So, of course, do women."

~ Beth Kephart, National Book Award Finalist and author of thirteen books, both fiction and nonfiction including, most recently, *You Are My Only*

"Before reading Anna Lefler's book, I had no idea that the word 'herpes-ish' even existed. Now I can't stop using it. This book is guaranteed to be passed around to all your friends. It's totally herpes-ish. But in a good way."

~ Jenny Lawson, The Bloggess and author of the forthcoming *Let's Pretend This Never Happened: A Mostly True Memoir* from Amy Einhorn Books

The
CHICKtionary

*From A-Line to Z-Snap, the Words
Every Woman Should Know*

INCLUDES 450+ WORDS NO WOMAN CAN LIVE WITHOUT!

ANNA LEFLER

AVON, MASSACHUSETTS

Published by
Adams Media, a division of F+W Media, Inc.
57 Littlefield Street, Avon, MA 02322. U.S.A.
www.adamsmedia.com

ISBN-10: 1-4405-2984-1
ISBN-13: 978-1-4405-2984-9
eISBN-10: 1-4405-3122-6
eISBN-13: 978-1-4405-3122-4

Printed in the United States of America.

10   9   8   7   6   5   4   3   2   1

Library of Congress Cataloging-in-Publication Data
is available from the publisher.

This book is available at quantity discounts for bulk purchases.
For information, please call 1-800-289-0963.

For Dan, Madison, and Henry
And for women everywhere

INTRODUCTION

It has been said that women and men come from two different planets. This theory would explain a lot, beginning with the language barrier. For eons, the two sexes have sat across from each other at the negotiating table like haggard diplomats, hammering out rudimentary common meaning between two fundamentally different methods of communication. As earnest as these efforts are, sometimes we can't help but feel we've fallen into the stereotypical tourist mindset, believing that all will be understood if we speak loudly and sloooowly.

In the meantime, women have created a complex and nuanced lexicon of their own, one that is effortlessly understood by all females and which conveys—through context, subtext and, occasionally, pretext—the ever-changing and largely annoying experience of being a contemporary earth woman. Like a secret handshake among lodge members, female dialect conveys volumes of unspoken meaning requiring no explanation, thus saving valuable conversation time that would be better spent critiquing someone's acid-washed jeggings.

For instance: You're considering cutting your own bangs? To the untrained ear, this is small talk, a throwaway comment. We, however, hear this as the distress call it is and have our purses and car keys in hand before you've finished your sentence.

And that's just the beginning.

Your new bra showcases your back fat? You're experiencing man drought, or—worse—your new relationship is laced with residual girlfriend? Troublesome T-zone? Depressed about your cankles? *We get it.*

That's not to say the female vernacular can be picked up overnight. For the non-native speaker—the one who thinks an espadrille is something found in a toolbox—fluency may come only after years of study. Sure, you'll experience frustrations along the way as you struggle to understand the subtle shadings between a cougar and a puma, but you'll enjoy deeply rewarding moments as well, like when you explain to your coworkers over fried potato skins the significant difference between secondary virginity and revirginization. For those seeking immersion in and understanding of the not-so-secret language of women, we hope you will come to think of *The Chicktionary* not only as a reference book soon to grace the shelves of America's finer vocational schools, but as your personal Rosetta Stone.

Far from being simply a phrase book for the male adventurer hoping to speak the lingo to the female locals, *The Chicktionary* is a critical text for women as well. For those seeking an efficient term to replace the cumbersome "that woman your jerk of a daddy deserted us for" (we suggest "stepwife"), or girlfriends looking to settle an argument regarding pubic topiary and the difference between the Sphinx and the landing strip, *The Chicktionary* stands ready to serve as the soon-to-be-dog-eared compendium of choice.

Whether you just got a Brazilian blowout at the salon, or you think that's something that happens to a rental car in Rio, there is much to be learned about the society of women—not to mention society at large—by taking a look at the feminine terminology that erupts and endures over time. In this easy-to-use volume (which has been alphabetized for convenience and freshness), you will find everyday words with their underlying meanings disclosed, as well as examples of contemporary female patois that you will no doubt be passing off as your own by dinnertime.

Beyond a mere collection of words and phrases, however, *The Chicktionary* is above all a celebration of a rich linguistic tapestry that is as familiar and comforting as your fat pants.

A

A-line, *adjective*

This term describes a skirt, dress, or similar garment whose silhouette flares out from the waist, becoming wider toward the hem and creating a shape that resembles both the letter "A" and a teepee, although, for some reason, the term "teepee-line" never caught on. Fitted at the waist and relaxed everywhere else, the A-line silhouette is both flattering to most figures and comfortable to wear. More importantly, however, the A-line will not divulge your figure flaws no matter how much it is waterboarded, unlike other garments that will happily sell your secrets all over town (*see also:* pencil skirt).

Aberzombie, *noun*

Derived from the name of the popular clothing stores, Aberzombie refers to any of the nation of plaid shirt-and-tank-top-wearing undead that can be seen staggering through the food courts of malls across America. Chillingly uniform in their short-shorts and matching expressions of disdain, the Aberzombies are young, camera-ready, and intent on finding WiFi. Note: if an Aberzombie does not respond to your attempts at conversation, it may be that she is suffering from short-term hearing loss having just lurched out of one of the stores during a deafening Willow Smith song.

Acrylic Nails, *noun*
Artificial fingernails made of activated acrylic powder that are applied on top of natural nails and, if done correctly, are tough enough to pull the screws right out of a fence. Acrylic nails are applied and maintained by a professional (*see also:* fill) and, depending on this person's skill level, the end result can vary in appearance from deceptively natural to aggressively mutant. Although the acrylic nails themselves are extremely durable, the harshness of the chemical application process takes a significant toll on the natural nails underneath and, once the acrylics are removed, leaves said nails about as sturdy as a dragonfly's wings.

Aftershave, *noun*
Used interchangeably with the term "men's cologne," aftershave is governed by the same rules as women's cologne when it comes to the quantity applied. These rules can be summed up in the following easy-to-remember phrase: "Less is more . . . and more is just wrong." Women are divided on men's wearing of cologne. While some find it alluring, others feel it reflects a tendency toward vanity that they find off-putting. There are also women who prefer wearing men's cologne to women's, which confuses everyone in the supermarket checkout line.

Alpha Girl, *noun*
Derived from the term "alpha dog," which refers to the lead dog within the social structure of the dog pack, alpha girl describes a

female who exhibits similar behaviors in the areas of leadership, status, and goal orientation while also maintaining a shiny, healthy coat. Although some may erroneously confuse the alpha girl with the queen bee (*see also:* queen bee), others liken her behaviors to those of a male in that she pursues her own agenda while disregarding the "rules" of typical female social groups. *Woof.*

Annual Exam, *noun*

The annual exam is an important medical assessment of your lady nethers which, depending on your doctor, may include multiple choice, fill-in-the-blank, and essay questions. Many women find the annual exam to be a stressful experience, which is unfortunate because this appointment offers several benefits that are often over-looked. These include: 1) the chance to milk the appointment for a half-day off from work (particularly if you have a male boss), 2) a block of uninterrupted time in which to catch up on reading *Yacht Management Magazine* in the company of cranky strangers, and 3) the opportunity to make the most of those stirrups by pretending you're a beautiful princess riding your faithful palomino into the enchanted forest where Prince Charming awaits. Or, you know, something to that effect.

Anorexic, *adjective*

Although this adjective is derived from the name of the serious and potentially fatal eating disorder anorexia nervosa, it is often used by women as a compliment. For instance, if your friend is fretting that her cocktail dress makes her look chubby, the comment, "Are you kidding? It's perfect—you look anorexic!" would be met with smiles and thanks. It's worth noting that the disease-as-compliment construction seen here is extremely rare and, as of this writing, it is still considered bad form to tell someone that her new jeans make her look "herpes-ish" or "gall-stoned."

Aqua Net, *noun*

There is hair spray . . . and then there is Aqua Net. Legendary shellac of the rich and famous as well as the merely mortal, Aqua Net carries with it the commercial mythology of female power in many forms, from the sleek prowess of the executive assistant to the big-haired sass of the pageant contestant to the sultry allure of today's cougar. For decades, Aqua Net's iconic spray can has been toted in train cases (*see also:* train case), placed on bathroom counters, and proudly displayed at hairdressers' workstations across America. Plus, the name subtly evokes some kind of waterborne superhero, and when you're trying to get your hair to stay put in a high-humidity situation, that's all good.

Aunt Flo, *proper noun*

1. A humorous nickname for your monthly period (*see also:* the curse, Festival of Menses). In addition to the entertainment value offered by the "flo/flow" homonym, the Aunt Flo code name for menstruation can be employed either when there are b-o-y-s within earshot or when the speaker is of such a delicate disposition that the use of the coarser "period" would be unthinkable. Note: you may not substitute another relative for "Flo" in this construction, because if you say you're bloated due to your Aunt Agatha being in town, no one will know what the hell you're talking about. **2.** Your mother's sister Florence.

B

Baby Bump, *noun*

Also known simply as "bump," this term refers to a woman's visible pregnancy bulge. A common term among tabloid reporters and paparazzi, baby bump is used most often in reference to celebrities. Examples of this use include, "Grammy-winner Alicia Keys showed off her baby bump in a beaded, Empire-waisted sheath," and "Paris Hilton's alleged baby bump was revealed to be nothing more than the aftermath of a Super Burrito." Although a campaign was launched recently to take the focus off of women's tummies and redirect scrutiny to male celebrities' midsections, the terms "beer bump" and "bratwurst bump" have yet to catch on.

Baby Shower, *noun*

A ritualized gathering during which a pregnant woman is given gifts while being closely scrutinized by female friends and acquaintances. May involve "games" (*see also:* hazing) and, for everyone's safety, had *better* involve food and drink. Baby shower guests instinctively group into two herds: those who have had a baby and those who have not. Within the herd of existing mothers, you can expect a palpable tension to emerge as the women who favor natural childbirth square off against those who prefer the use of pain-blocking methods such as the epidural. A skilled hostess will monitor the rising aggression levels in both herds as guests' various emotional issues emerge and, just as the shower is approaching flash point, will discharge the tension with the words, "Cake time!"

Bachelor Party, *noun*
A ritualistic gathering held in advance of a wedding during which the groom-to-be is celebrated and the honor of his future wife is upheld through all manner of drink, dance, and general revelry. The bachelor party is traditionally an all-male event with the single exception of the female exotic dancer hired by the best man to perform. Without fail, the male partygoers become charmed by this young med student and soon lose interest in her performance, forming a protective circle of chairs around her and spending the balance of the evening either helping her prepare for her upcoming midterms or taking turns reading aloud from Jane Austen's *Pride and Prejudice.*

Bachelorette Party, *noun*
A spectacularly tasteless night of public debauchery prior to a wedding during which the bride-to-be is accompanied about town by her friends, maid of honor, and bridesmaids as she absorbs as much alcohol as she can possibly hold while aggressively pursuing intercourse with as many strange men as she can find. In keeping with time-honored tradition, the night's celebration is marked by rampant vulgarity, spontaneous nudity, and copious puking, preferably on the

street or out the sunroof of a moving limousine. Also, everyone talks about how awesome the groom is.

Back Fat, *noun*
First documented and named by bridal pioneers in the early nineties, back fat is an insidious layer of poofy flab that can be found oozing across the backs and lower shoulders of most adult women. Extremely difficult to camouflage even in its least-advanced stages, back fat becomes corralled into drifts in the presence of bra straps and other constrictions, resulting in an archipelago of unattractive lumps that are visible under even the most reinforced knitwear.

Back Hair, *noun*
Back hair presents yet another set of axes along which women as a population can be divided. For instance, there is the group of women who would never consider being with a man who has a hairy back. Then there is the group who would consider it, but only on the condition that the man address the condition via regular, professional waxing. Further, there are those women who do not care for back hair, but worry about hurting the man's feelings by mentioning their preference. Lastly, there are the women who actively seek out men with hairy backs.

Fun*fact* You could fit this last group into a pup tent.

Backrub, *noun*
1. A soothing, therapeutic massage of the shoulders and/or back that is ideally administered by a trained professional, but can also be quite pleasurable when given by a sincere, motivated amateur (preferably neither an employee of yours nor the person who signs *your* paycheck). **2.** When placed in quotation marks, "backrub" takes on a different shade of meaning, namely an excuse for a man to apply his hands to you in the hopes that his skillful caress will work you into such a lather of desire that he'll soon be penning one of those *Penthouse Forum* letters.

Bag Hag, *noun*
More flatteringly known as a "purse enthusiast," the bag hag is a woman who tirelessly and annoyingly pursues a state of perfect handbag self-actualization through aggressive acquisition of every "it bag" that comes on the market. A willing slave to the whims of designer supply-and-demand, the bag hag happily announces that her man Silvio at Barneys just bumped her up on the wait list for the new Balenciaga. In contrast, a self-proclaimed bag hag is simply a woman who loves purses, but knows her limitations and is satisfied to worship the objects of her affection from afar.

Baked a Cake on Your Face, *phrase*
This phrase is a clever and accurate description of the condition in which, at a certain point during the day, your makeup combines with your face's natural oils and creates an undesirable sheen that looks remarkably like the residue left behind when you remove a freshly baked cake layer from its pan. Although no amount of flour applied prior to makeup application will prevent the so-called

"cake-face effect" if a woman's skin is predisposed to it, recent advancements in oil-absorption technology (*see also:* blotting sheets) reduce this unwanted pastry shine to a soft, sugar-free glow.

BAM!, *exclamation*

Popularized by television chef Emeril Lagasse, this extremely versatile expression can mean anything from "Wow!" to "Fabulous!" to "*That's* right!" to "Sniff it, loser!" Not to be confused with the graphic sound effect seen on the classic *Batman* television series starring Adam West, today's BAM! carries a broader range of meanings. Note these contrasting examples: "You should have seen Juanita at last night's party—she was head-to-toe BAM!" versus "Here comes the boss and Jerome still isn't at his desk. BAM!"

Banana Hammock, *noun*

Outside the world of competitive swimming (and Europe), most women just don't know what to do with a man who voluntarily goes out in public in a tiny little Speedo-style swimsuit. To deal with this discomfort, we make up nicknames for the suit. Like seal-a-meal. And grape smuggler. It's not meant maliciously, honest. On the contrary, we give men a lot of credit for having the balls (which we can totally see, by the way) to wear the revealing swimsuit instead of the safer baggy surf trunks. We admit that we might be a tad envious of the fact that men aren't expected to undergo the extensive and harrowing hair-removal processes that we do in order to be considered "swimsuit-ready" (*see also:* Brazilian wax). Nor, if the local beaches and community pools are providing accurate data, is there an apparent fitness requirement.

Bandeau, *noun*

From the French word meaning "there's no way that's staying up," this is a type of woman's top that consists of a strip of fabric encircling the chest at breast level and remaining aloft through snugness and prayers. Most often seen as the upper portion of a women's two-piece swimsuit, the bandeau top's unique squishing-flattening action gives it the ability to make even the perkiest, most voluptuous bustline look like a tube sock full of wet sand. A bonus feature of the bandeau is its ability to shift from a top to a sassy belt when it interacts with even the slightest amount of pool or ocean water.

Bangs, *noun*

An enigmatic fringe of hair that hangs from the top of the face and whose sole purpose is to remind you how much you love either the hairstyle you *used* to have or the hairstyle you *will* have once your frickin' bangs grow out. Bangs are available in four lengths: 1) too short, 2) too long, 3) awkward, and 4) in your eyes like tiny knives. Much like donating an organ or changing your will, the decision to cut bangs is generally acknowledged as one that should be acted upon only after a period of deep introspection and personal reflection, as well as consultation with clergy and/or a professional hairstylist—one whom you *generously* tipped on your last salon visit.

Basset Knees, *noun*

A heartbreaking condition in which one's knees exhibit multiple wrinkles and a general bagginess that serves to draw the observer's eye away from your cute outfit, smart shoes, and kicky handbag in a manner that is most damning to your mojo. Named for the layers of thick wrinkles that are the hallmark of the adorable basset breed, basset knees are, interestingly, the opposite of adorable. Stubborn in the extreme, basset knees are resistant to nutritional and physical fitness regimens of all kinds, often holding out to be the very last features on your body to become toned. In fact, a West Virginia woman was once exhumed in order to settle a legal matter and investigators were shocked to find the coffin empty with the exception of a pair of basset knees, which family members later identified as belonging to the woman in question.

Bat Wings, *noun*
Undulating curtains of flab that hang from the underside of your arms between the elbows and the armpits. The appearance of bat wings can be a startling occurrence during a routine activity, such as reaching to adjust your rearview mirror and discovering that you look like a flying squirrel frantically leaping from one treetop to the next. Notoriously stealthy, bat wings can strike at any time and in any age group. As they are naturally unyielding when confronted with traditional exercise and other toning and firming methods, their only effective treatment remains the application of sleeves. Long ones.

Beach Hair, *noun*
The coastal equivalent of bed head, beach hair is another of those mythical hair arrangements that strives to look spontaneous, but in fact requires a team of scalp wranglers and a bucket full of specialized products to achieve. The term "soft waves" occurs repeatedly in discussions on the topic of beach hair, as do sexy words like "tousled" and "wild." These are in stark contrast to the words we use to describe *our* hair after a day at the beach—words like "matted"

and "bent." Perhaps we're going to the wrong beach, because after a day of getting bashed by waves, rubbing sunscreen in our eyes, and flicking wet sand out of our butt seams, our appearance is less suited to cocktails and smooth jazz at Ken's Malibu beach house than to being airlifted out by the Coast Guard.

Beauty Mark, *noun*
A petite mole that is considered a desirable visual enhancement (most often on females) if ideally placed on the face, neck, shoulder, or breast. The ability of the well-placed beauty mark to draw positive attention to one's attributes is sometimes duplicated by the use of artificial beauty marks in the form of stick-on shapes or dots that are applied with dark eyeliner or other cosmetics. It's worth noting that not just any natural mole will cut it as a beauty mark. Unfortunate placement, troubling protuberance, overly sufficient acreage, or general wooliness take the mole out of the category of beauty mark and place it instead in the category of things you should have checked by your dermatologist.

Bedazzler, *noun*
An ingenious device that attaches metal studs and rhinestones to anything you can wrangle between its jaws. Driven to household-name status by its catchy television ads, this crafts item unleashed a kaleidoscope of custom-embellished T-shirts, jackets, and tote bags when it was introduced to consumers in the seventies. Since then, literally millions of T-shirts have been returned to their rightful owners, thanks to their names being spelled out in sparkles across the front.

Bed Head, *noun*

1. A studied, highly manipulated hairstyle that seeks to mimic how you imagine your hair would look if you'd spent the night having hot, high-def sex with a starlet/young gun, then rolled out of the thousand-thread-count sack just in time to effortlessly throw on your vintage motorcycle jacket before heading to the impossibly quaint farmer's market where you thoughtfully finger the produce while radiating hot, high-def sex. **2.** The misshapen crime scene that greets you from the top of your head each and every morning and which has the capacity to frighten both children and livestock.

Ben Wa Balls, *noun*

In use among a variety of cultures for centuries, Ben Wa balls and the like are instruments of female sexual arousal as well as tools used to help increase the strength of the vaginal muscles. The balls can be made of a variety of materials and hollow models can contain smaller spheres or even chimes. (Was that the doorbell?) The balls are inserted into the vagina (the anus is another option when seeking erotic stimulation), where they remain until removed using an optional retrieval cord or are coughed or sneezed out. For erotic stimulation, a gentle rocking motion is recommended, although Mr. Wa has reportedly received complaints that the balls' effect is too subtle to be felt. For conditioning of the vaginal muscles, the balls are held inside the vagina with a clenching motion, taking the definition of "private training" to its extreme.

Bestie, *noun*

An adorable name for a best friend, notably a *current* best friend. A woman may have multiple besties, such as a work bestie, school bestie, etc. The bestie relationship is slightly more casual than the best friend relationship and is at least a level below your best friend for life (*see also:* biffle) on the official friend hierarchy. It's worth noting that the female friendship hierarchy is a fluid construct that is highly sensitive to subtle shifts in tone and circumstance as well as the spontaneous creation of new levels and names thereof. That being said, this is what bestie means. At least for today.

Beta Baby, *noun*
The heavily scrutinized first child born into a circle of female friends. The beta baby provokes a spectrum of reactions among group members, ranging from fascination and affection to annoyance and naked envy, depending on the friend's current marital and/or relationship status and the degree to which the beta baby disrupts the group. Although scientists work to pioneer methods for testing the resilience of the female friendship dynamic, it is unlikely that a more effective instrument than the beta baby will ever be developed.

Bias Cut, *adjective*
This term describes a garment—typically a longer skirt or dress—that is made on the diagonal, maximizing the stretch and drape of the fabric. Used to the greatest effect on lightweight materials, the technique of cutting on the bias creates a slight elasticity that maximizes the fabric's ability to hug the body and accentuate its curves.

Fun*fact* The bias cut technique also creates a garment that will cling to every bulge, pooch, (*see also:* pooch), ripple, dimple, and pucker on your figure, thus broadcasting all your issues to the world at large.

Biffle, *noun*

Variation of BFFL, or best friend for life. Your biffle is your home-girl, your wingwoman (*see also:* wingwoman), the top of the female friendship hierarchy—and you are the same for her. Your biffle knows where you hide your spare key, the home address of the guy who landed you in the women's clinic with those nasty red bumps, and the real story behind that thing that happened that time at the cabin. Not even your kryptonite guy (*see also:* kryptonite guy) can destabilize the bond you share with your biffle.

Bikini, *noun*

Invented by a French engineer and named for the Bikini Atoll in the Pacific, the bikini is an especially skimpy version of the two-piece swimsuit (*see also:* two-piece) and, let's face it, the mainstream hot-ness yardstick by which all other women's swimsuits are judged. Beyond the basic bikini model, there are subcategories such as the cheeky, thong, and g-string bikinis that raise the suit's level of dif-ficulty by winnowing away even more of its fabric. Though its exact elastic boundaries may ebb and flow as the seasons pass, the bikini, once considered scandalous, is destined to remain as much of a fix-ture on the beach as the hot dog-swiping seagulls and the lone hairy guy in the Speedo.

Biological Clock, *noun*

A popular term for the supposed internal timing mechanism that drives a woman to begin actively desiring a baby. Although each woman's body operates on its own individual timeframe, popular culture dictates that a woman begins to become aware of the "tick-ing" of her clock in her late twenties and early thirties. It is further theorized that the ticking becomes more pronounced as the woman moves through her mid-thirties, and some claim that it can ratchet up to an audible beeping as the fortieth birthday approaches. Is there a snooze button? Yes, and it can be activated by eating at any children's so-called "theme restaurant," particularly on a Saturday.

Birth Control Pills, *noun*
Commonly known as "the pill," these oral contraceptives began to be available in all fifty states in the mid-sixties, thus kicking off the sexual revolution and giving ladies one more thing to carry in that secret zippered compartment inside their handbags. Birth control pills are used by more than 100 million women worldwide, most of whom are standing in line at a pharmacy right now, wondering what the hell is taking so long.

> **Fun*fact*** There are many formulations of birth control pills, and the ones that do *not* mesh well with your particular body chemistry can bring on the kinds of exciting side effects that will have your friends backing slowly away from you and your loved ones checking the lock on the gun cabinet.

Bitch Lit, *noun*
The tough, motorcycle-jacket-wearing sister of chick lit (*see also:* chick lit), bitch lit doesn't vent about her bad date in loopy cursive on the pages of her fuzzy pink diary. Instead, she reaches across the table, grabs the man in question by his shirt, and spells it out to his face before stalking out and hailing a cab. Bitch lit, with its edgy anti-heroines and sharp satire, focuses less on romance and more

on power—specifically, power in the hands of women who have no qualms about wielding it.

Black Shoes, *noun*

"Why do you have so many pairs of black shoes?" Only a Philistine would ask such a question, and it reveals a troubling fashion short-sightedness that, if we're honest with ourselves, heralds the beginning of the end of this relationship. Ah, well, it was nice while it lasted, although we won't miss that canvas belt you seemed to be so attached to, nor will we be sorry never again to lay eyes on that shiny shirt with the diagonal diamonds that you thought made you look like "The Situation." No, you never admitted it directly, but that time we surprised you in the bedroom wearing the shirt and looking at yourself in the mirror over the tops of your sunglasses? Yeah, we knew.

Blind Date, *noun*

For those in need of a reminder that our species is one, ultimately, of supreme optimism, consider the blind date. You select your clothing with care, then launch a multitiered grooming frenzy that includes all the usual efforts as well as some "special occasion" rituals such as strategic shaving and cotton-swabbing. You perhaps apply the lightest mist/smack of a favorite fragrance, check your look in the mirror one last time, and then head out into the romantic wilderness to meet a mystery person—one who may end up sharing the rest of your life with you, but whom at least you hope doesn't spend the majority of the night digging in his or her ear with a pinky. In a society overflowing with crass pessimism, there are few things more beautiful than the naïve, ever-replenishing hope of the blind date. Stupid, yes. But beautiful nonetheless.

Bling, *noun*
A term for jewelry of any and all kind. Short for the more formal "bling-bling," the term originated in rap culture as a play on the imaginary sound that light makes when it strikes a highly reflective surface such as a diamond, precious metal, or even a blinding smile. After moving into mainstream culture, where it was neutered through widespread overuse, bling lost all its street cred and became a subtle, tongue-in-cheek expression for those who continued to use it.

Bloat, *noun*
Officially known as "the bloat," this is an uncomfortable distension of the belly and other components of your digestive system resulting from eating—or in some cases even *thinking* about eating—something you shouldn't. A related malady, known as "the dread bloat," is triggered not by food but rather by the waxing and waning of the hormonal tide that accompanies the monthly Festival of Menses (*see also:* Aunt Flo, the curse). In extreme instances, both forms of bloat can move beyond their usual boundaries and encompass the entire body, making everything from your hair follicles to your toenail cuticles feel as though they're about to blow.

Blotting Sheets, *noun*
Ingenious, portable sheets of absorbent material that, when applied, suck the oily shine right off your face and leave in its place an appealing, matte surface. Blotting sheets typically are comprised of

naturally absorbent paper and tissue fibers, although some are made from nontissue microfilm. (Note: no one understands exactly how the film ones work—since when is something rubbery also absorbent? *Weird.*) Anyway, because, according to popular decree, certain parts of you are supposed to be shiny (eyes, eyelids, lips, hair) and other parts of you are *not* supposed to be shiny (*see also:* baked a cake on your face), blotting sheets may be the perfect solution for maintaining your critical shine–no shine ratio.

Blue Ball, *verb*
To produce prolonged sexual arousal in a man but deny him the ultimate satisfaction of achieving orgasm, thus bringing the cycle of arousal to its normal completion (*see also:* tease). Blue balling a man, or creating what is officially termed vasocongestion, is said to produce testicular pain although there is very little medical research that confirms these complaints. It is suggested, however, that the condition can be relieved with anti-inflammatory drugs, which puts an entirely new spin on the vintage expression, "Take two aspirin and call me in the morning."

Board Shorts, *noun*
Women's board shorts—based on men's swim trunks but marketed to females—have removed one of the main obstacles keeping many women on the sand and out of the surf: the women's swimsuit. It's true that everyone on the beach is, in fact, looking at your butt when you walk out to the water, and we know it. Who needs that pressure? Styled with the comfort and wearability of regular shorts, this is one swimsuit bottom that you'll never have to keep delicately yanking out of your butt crease. Women's board shorts are second

only to jeans in waist-down coverage and much easier to swim in than wet denim.

Booty, *noun*
A popular slang term for butt, used most often in reference to a woman's posterior, which is, according to a number of sources, built for shaking. Beyond its basic meaning, booty conveys a playfully complimentary tone while implying a strong sexual attraction to said derriere on the part of the speaker. Immortalized in the hit song "Bootylicious" by Beyoncé, the prevalence of this term in popular culture shows no signs of diminishing in the near future. May also be pronounced "boo-TAY" for added effect and reinforcement of 'liciousness.

Booty Call, *noun*
A spontaneous call, text, or other form of instantaneous communication with someone you know but are not in a relationship with for the purpose of having no-strings-attached sex. One step removed from the "friends with benefits" arrangement (*see also:* friends with benefits), the booty call can be placed to someone outside the category of friend. In fact, many feel that the booty call is best suited to those on the periphery of one's social circle as this encourages the mental compartmentalization required for both parties to emerge from the coupling unfettered by collateral emotional attachment. This lack of attachment is the foundation of the booty call and any thoughts of sleeping over, notions of catching a matinee together, or internal musings on the way his bangs scatter across his forehead should serve as red flags that you are departing booty call territory.

Bosom, *noun*

The unsexiest word for breasts ever coined, "bosom" connotes a distinctly grandmother-ish vibe, with the unexpected twist of suggesting that your grandmother is frickin' *stacked*. Often used in the context of tucking something or someone to your bosom, the term implies nonsexual comfort-giving and nurturing with the understanding that there is more than ample cushioning available for such activities. In contrast, it is unlikely that you will hear a reference to "tucking someone to your ribcage" outside the world of competitive wrestlers and skydiving instructors.

Botox, *noun*

A hugely popular substance that, although derived from a neurotoxin, exhibits an epic capacity for beautification when injected into, say, that troublesome double-gulley between your eyebrows (*see also:* elevens). Initially used most often by women over the age of forty, Botox is now popular among women in their twenties and thirties as well. As with any cosmetic procedure, the potential for overzealous treatment exists, which can result in a temporary inability to create facial expressions that correspond to such overrated emotions as surprise, fear, anger, and joy (*see also:* smize).

Brazilian Blowout, *noun*

A professionally applied heat and chemical treatment that fundamentally alters your hair texture and leaves you looking more like Jennifer Aniston and less like a labradoodle. Although concerns have been raised about the potential health hazards of exposure to the harsh chemicals used in the straightening process, it is widely acknowledged that most women would happily run through a hail of gunfire to have silky, carefree hair for three straight months. The Brazilian blowout is similar to the Japanese hair straightening process, but the latter does not leave you with an irresistible impulse to dance in the streets wearing nothing but a thong and a feather headdress.

Brazilian Wax, *noun*
Introduced in New York in 1987, the Brazilian bikini wax (*see also:* the Hollywood, the Sphinx, and the full Monty) is somewhat misunderstood in that it is not necessarily defined by the removal of *all* pubic hair, but rather the removal of all pubic hair around the labia and further back, including a thorough denuding of the area known to estheticians as "the basement." In other words, contrary to popular belief, you can have a Brazilian and keep a small doormat on your front porch, but everything on the back porch has got to go.

Breakup, *noun*
The dissolution of a romantic relationship that results in a variety of emotional reactions ranging from devastation to glee. There are two kinds of breakups: 1) those initiated by him, and 2) those initiated by you. Both kinds of breakups are his fault, and anyone who doesn't *get* that obviously hasn't been reading your blog. Some people claim there is a third category of breakup—the so-called "mutual" breakup—but those of us who have been around the block more than once know that this mythical concept should be filed under "U" for "Unicorn" (*see also:* remaining friends, hatred and retribution).

Breast Implants, *noun*

Prostheses that are surgically inserted for the purposes of breast reconstruction or aesthetic enhancement. Breast implants consist of pillow-like bladders of silicone, saline, or other alternative fillers that are positioned within the layers of breast and muscle tissue based on a woman's specific body structure and requirements. With respect to reconstruction, advancements in implant technology and surgery have been an immeasurable help to women recovering from mastectomies and similar surgeries. On the aesthetic enhancement side, the proliferation of implant surgeries for cosmetic enhancement have spawned an entirely new category of social debate as both men and women attempt to distinguish natural breasts from those that have been augmented.

Brick House, *noun*

1. A woman who is judged to be voluptuous, "stacked," or otherwise aggressively curvaceous. Variant of the term "brick shithouse," the use of this description implies a well-built sturdiness that might not sound terribly complimentary but is widely regarded as such. **2.** Title of the Commodores' hit song from their eponymous 1977 album and arguably one of the best funk songs of all time. In fact, it has been proven in international studies that if you can stand completely still while listening to "Brick House," you are clinically dead and/or a big party buzzkill.

Bridal Gown, *noun*

It is impossible to overstate the expectations that are loaded onto this typically white garment. The bridal gown is called upon to make you look chic but approachable, hot but loyal, slim but never skeletal, sexy but with motherhood potential, *au courant* but classic, playful but substantial, and on and on. Then you have to consider your wedding theme (Renaissance? Evening in Paris? Enviro-friendly? Beer?) and somehow mash your gown into that category as well. When all of these factors (and many, *many* more) are taken into account, it suddenly becomes clear why you can't walk two feet in a bridal store without tripping over a box of tissues.

Bridal Headpiece, *noun*
The opportunities for fashion missteps when selecting the bridal gown are miniscule when compared to those that must be navigated on the bumpy road to a headpiece. Apparently there's something about things that go on your head that makes even the most down-to-earth bride decide the time has come to let her fashion freak flag fly. Since when does your sister the metalhead like pillbox hats with veils? Who knew your best friend had an Isis complex? And why is your normally level-headed business partner swooning over the organza headband attached to a silk flower/feather meteor the size of a trash can lid?

Bridesmaid, *noun*
Dependable foot soldier of the bridal army and under the command of both bride and maid of honor, the bridesmaid is one of the unsung heroes of Operation Wedding. (And, no, those faux-pearl earrings that you cheaped out on—the ones whose "steel" posts corroded everyone's ears within a week—do not come close to repaying your bridesmaids for putting up with your diva antics.) Much like a devoted golden retriever, the bridesmaid allows you to dress her up funny, send her to fetch things, and make her listen to you blab

on for hours while remaining a loyal, good-natured companion to the end.

Bridesmaid's Dress, *noun*

The garment chosen by the bride for the bridesmaids to wear in the wedding ceremony with, some posit, the specific intent of making the bridesmaids look like frumpy, misshapen washouts (*see also:* butt bow). As with many aspects of life, the key to successful selection of the bridesmaid's dress is plausible deniability and, as a bride, there's no time like the present to work on your game face. It's not enough simply to select a mint green tiered chiffon turtleneck dress with fringed bell sleeves for your nearest and dearest friends to wear; you have to *sell* it. Once they've mirrored your perceived enthusiasm back to you, then you can forever claim that the dress was a "group decision" and you can get on with the business of selecting the appropriate ostrich-feather hat to go with it.

Bridezilla, *noun*

A popular term coined in reference to a bride whose ego, antics, and diva-like behavior have gotten so out of control that she has become a menace to society and may need to be taken out by a squadron of tiny fighter planes filmed against a blue screen. Sure, it can be difficult not to get swept up in the excitement of the wedding planning, most of which is focused on you, your dreams, and your vision. (Okay, stuff like that. "Your vision." You have to knock that off right now.) It's important to remember, however, that the wedding is not *just* about you, it's also about what's-his-face.

Briet, *noun*

A diet undertaken by a woman specifically for the purpose of losing weight prior to her wedding. Created by combining the words "bride" and "diet" (not, unfortunately, "brie" and the letter "t"), the very coining of this term underscores just how much pressure is on today's bride to show up looking like a million bucks at her nuptials (which hopefully carry a price tag somewhere south of that figure). Depending on how invested the bride is in the goal of perfecting her figure for her wedding day, she may begin her briet regimen anywhere from a week to twenty years prior to the blessed event.

Broad, *noun*

An archaic and disparaging term for a woman that is likely best known in popular culture through its association with both the Rat Pack and films of the noir genre. Broad is one of those negative terms that, once reclaimed by the group at whom it was originally aimed, becomes a form of lighthearted self-deprecation. Whereas decades ago, the labeling of a woman as a broad implied a coarseness that could, in its extreme, be taken as synonymous with prostitution, a contemporary woman who refers to herself as a broad implies instead that she has not limited herself to society's traditional definition of womanhood and could, if motivated, happily kick your scrawny ass, Bub.

Brooch, *noun*

Not to be confused with a pin, the brooch is the elder stateswoman of jewelry and is not about to take any guff from you, missy. Often paired with reinforced-toe stockings, the brooch can include pearls, jewels, rhinestones, enamel figures, and metal twigs or leaves. These items are formed into a conglomeration that, like a fist-sized satellite from a faraway, glitter-covered galaxy, perches on the lapel of a woman whose wardrobe features many lapels and dazzles all who behold it.

Bunny Boiler, *noun*

This term came into popularity following the release of the film *Fatal Attraction* and refers to someone who is dangerously obsessive (the insinuation being that this is a bad thing). In the movie, Alex—played by Glenn Close—takes extreme exception to being classified as a "fling" by the Michael Douglas character named Dan. (Apparently, she thinks of herself more as girlfriend material.) One of the many ways in which she shows her acute dissatisfaction with the whole arrangement is to kill Dan's daughter's beloved pet bunny and set him to boil in a pot on the family stove. Sure, Alex comes off looking pretty bad there, but it's important to remember that she also tries to stab the guy, which we can all agree is definitely worse.

Butt Bow, *noun*

Hallmark of the bridesmaid's dress, the butt bow is the scourge of the dressmaking industry and has been blamed over the years for everything from reception brawls to honeymoon impotence. Varying in size from a boogie board to a hang glider, the butt bow is typically fashioned from the same industrial-grade nylon as the rest of the dress, but can also be made from tulle, lace, or—if you really want to sever some relationships—organza. Regardless of the fabric or color, however, the butt bow must perform its primary function: to make the wearer appear twenty to fifty pounds heavier than she actually is while conveying a tragic, spinsterish air that no amount of eyeliner can counteract.

Butt Bra, *noun*
Any of a variety of harness-like undergarments that use straps, elastic, or strategic openings to hoist your derriere to an altitude believed to be more attractive and appealing. Surely one of the more ingenious and hardworking items to be found in your underwear drawer (*see also:* foundation garment), the butt bra works on the same principle as the push-up bra, but instead relies on a "pulling" effect to lift and optimally position the bun cheeks. While the quest for further advancements in the field of butt-enhancement continues, the butt bra currently sits on the frontier of rump-perkiness technology.

Butt Protector, *noun*
Casual name for any garment worn for the sole purpose of hiding your rear end from view because you don't feel confident about its appearance. Butt protectors come in all forms, including long shirts, tunics, oversized T-shirts, and the popular sweatshirt-tied-around-the-waist. The butt-protector lifestyle can be adopted at any stage of life, but often emerges during periods of transition such as recovery from pregnancy, onset of age-related weight gain, or the temporary spread resulting from a nasty breakup. Are we fooling anyone? No. Do we know this? Yes.

C

Caftan, *noun*

For full-body camouflage, the caftan is hard to beat. Offering virtually impenetrable coverage from fingertips to toenails to jawline, the caftan obscures all of your figure flaws while making a style statement that's damn hard to ignore. Have even more to say? Well, then go for a caftan that expresses your individuality with unexpected pops of color, captivating patterns, and a sassy gold tassel on the zipper pull. Once available exclusively to the California/Florida retirement set, it is rumored that Angelina was recently photographed wearing one while breakfasting with Brad on the back porch of their French chateau.

Cameltoe, *noun*

The unfortunate visual result when snug pants or shorts ride up in the front and become visibly lodged between your labia (*see also:* ow), which prompts the question *if your pants are jammed that far up in your business, then where the hell is your underwear—in your ribcage?* The cameltoe is named for its uncanny resemblance to the forefoot of the camel (or "ship of the desert"), an animal that you might be interested to know is classified as an even-toed ungulate. Note: although "ungulate" sounds dirty, it's a perfectly legitimate and official science word.

Cankles, *noun*
The tragic lack of differentiation between calf and ankle that results when both segments of the leg are the same thickness. Also known as "tree trunk legs" or "pipeline pins," cankles can strike any age group with decidedly geriatric results. Although there is no remedy for cankles (the ankle-slenderizing workout DVDs recently hawked on late-night infomercials having been exposed as bogus), stylists recommend the vigorous application of ankle-strap shoes to create the illusion of two separate leg regions.

Capri Pants, *noun*
Much like espadrilles (*see also:* espadrilles), Capri pants evoke a specific mood based on a geographic location. Of course, there is no *actual* place called Capri, but if there were it would be unspeakably chic (*see also:* chic) and everyone would run around having clambakes on the beach and slinging perfect vodka Negronis on the decks of the hand-polished yachts moored in the cove and the suntanned men would wear kerchiefs knotted around their necks and that wouldn't look even a little bit stupid and the women would all wear cat's-eye sunglasses and take black-and-white candid photos of one another. Oh, and Capri pants hit just above the ankles, btw.

Carbs, *noun*
Short for carbohydrates, carbs are magically powerful food elements that seem to be omnipresent in any diet that is not limited to

sturgeon and cabbage leaves. Prized for their fat-retention qualities, carbs are the go-to compound for the woman who is terrified she might accidentally lose weight. Often disguised as healthy foods, such as beans and bananas, carbs can also be found in pretty much *anything* worth putting in your mouth. Once inside your system, carbs work hard to make sure your body holds on to each and every fat cell, ensuring that your beloved saddlebags, muffin tops, and pooch will continue to grace your figure for decades to come. There are currently several popular diets that outline low- or no-carb eating regimens and whose followers can often be found pressed up against the window of the local bakery.

Cellulite, *noun*
A universally despised condition in which skin takes on a "dimpled" or "effed-up" appearance due to—*oh, who the hell cares what causes it just get it off of us, man!* Anyway, cellulite (*see also:* cottage cheese) is one of those things that, once on you, is really hard to get rid of, kind of like cigarette smell or a car salesman. Although lasers and radiofrequency systems appear to be promising treatments to reduce cellulite, there is no reliable evidence that the many cosmetic creams and topical ointments currently on the market offer any improvement of this condition. (Especially the one you can buy through the catalog with the cute pink flowers on it. Trust us on this.)

CFM, *acronym*
This acronym, which stands for the unabashedly proactive "Come fuck me," refers to a particular category of women's shoes designed specifically to inflame male desire. Distinct from stripper shoes (*see also:* stripper shoes), CFMs are worn outside the professional arousal

arena. Hallmarks of CFMs can include: 1) exceptionally tall stiletto heels, 2) an excess of bondage-style straps, 3) the presence of multiple buckles or other metallic accoutrements, 4) construction from a shiny material in the colors of red and/or black, and 5) a general, fierce pointy-ness. The CFM wields substantial fantasy-inducing power when encountered by the typical male psyche and can prove to be a considerable distraction in the workplace. Then again, depending on the mindset of the male in question, the definition of CFM can be expanded to include fuzzies, running shoes, and combat boots.

Chic, *adjective*

This is one of those words that you know is a compliment, but you're not quite comfortable using it because you can't be absolutely certain what it means. You know it's got something to do with being fashionable, but then things get a little fuzzy. There seems to be some magical yet indefinable quality inherent in the woman who earns the label of chic. What is it about this word? Its innate Frenchness . . . or the fact that it looks like a baby chicken but sounds like a brand of condoms? Or is it that this uniquely feminine word makes us a little insecure, wondering if we have what it takes to merit its application to us? Nah, we're pretty sure it's the French thing.

Chick Flick, *noun*

A delightful movie genre that seeks to satisfy the cinematic cravings of a broad female target audience by touching on certain universal themes believed to appeal to women. These themes may include, but are not limited to, the following: 1) turns out the male friend you're always confiding in is hawt, 2) what men really want is a bumbling neurotic, 3) what you really need is a great pair of strappy sandals, 4) you get bonus points for feisty, 5) it really helps to have a sassy immigrant family, 6) inside every woman is a supermodel just waiting for a montage/makeover to bring her out, 7) your prince will come—and chances are he'll be driving a luxury car.

Chick Lit, *noun*

A genre of women's commercial fiction that is most often lauded as "light" and "fun" while also criticized as "fluffy" and "a guilty pleasure." Chick lit stories tend to contain certain stock elements such as a wicked female boss, a wise-cracking sidekick, an obsession with fashion or shopping, and either a sought-after love interest or no-good ex (or both). Although often maligned by more "serious" authors, the chick lit genre continues to thrive because sometimes a girl just needs to throw back a cosmo and live vicariously through Bridget Jones as she gets her mitts on that tasty Mr. Darcy.

Chicken Cutlet, *noun*

A nickname for a freestanding, adhesive bra cup worn with revealing clothing to eliminate the distraction of a visible, traditional bra. Typically purchased and worn in sets of two (one for each breast, on average), the chicken cutlet is made of spongy material and is applied to the underside of the breast, where it is held in place by special adhesive and lots of prayers. This term can also refer to inserts that are slipped into a traditional bra to add contour and fullness. The cutlet is named for its uncanny resemblance to an actual piece of chicken meat, which, by the way, causes nothing but trouble if stuffed into your shirt.

Childbirth, *noun*

Part miracle of nature, part slasher film, childbirth is one of those things that has to be experienced to be believed, particularly the first time around. Like skydiving, you can listen to the instructor talk all day long, but until someone pushes *your* ass out of an airplane, it's all academic. Luckily, every woman's body is slightly different, so no matter how experienced your doctor/midwife/cabdriver is, there will be a moment when he or she looks truly perplexed by something happening between your legs. It's comforting at that time to remember that women have been giving birth for centuries and the body knows what to do. After all, it's as simple as slipping a cannonball through a keyhole.

Chin Hair, *noun*

On a female, an unwanted and highly visible follicular sprout on or near the chin area that displays a remarkable capacity for catching both natural and artificial light. Contrary to popular belief, chin hairs—not the regular, microscopic kind, but rather the freakishly long kind that make you wonder if you've encountered a kink in your DNA strand that contains a stretch of catfish genes—can appear on a woman of any age. Erupting spontaneously and almost always when you are out in public, the chin hair settles in like a deadbeat relative who, even after forcible removal, can be counted on to show up again and again. It's worth noting that the most effective tool for locating these rogue hairs is your automobile's rearview mirror, especially when the sunroof is open.

Chip Clip, *noun*

Officially known as a "jaw clip," the chip clip is part tail fin, part bear trap. The chip clip clamps onto a wad of hair, gripping it in its spidery jaws and holding it securely as its high-profile "handle" towers above the hairdo like the topknot of an exotic bird. It is this portion of the chip clip that transmits style signals to others in the vicinity. Is your clip fancy (covered with glitter or sequins), wild (printed with zebra stripes or some other animal-skin pattern), or elegant (drawing a blank on that one)? More importantly, does it accentuate your feather earrings? Let's hope so.

Classic Pieces, *noun*

Apparently, we're all supposed to be wearing these, but what are they? Often modified with the words "timeless" and "elegant," the concept also can appear in conjunction with the ominous phrase "investment piece." Is this some kind of code? Should we be down-loading an Audrey Hepburn app or something? As usual, the fashion industry gives us no clear guidelines. We know, for instance, that a white T-shirt is considered a classic piece, but does it matter which band's album cover is on the front?

Cleanser/Cleaner, *noun*

Is it us? Has anyone else noticed the sly use of the word "cleanser" on cosmetic and skincare products? What's up with that? You have to admit, it does sound a little nicer to say "facial cleanser." Some-how the loss of that "s" turns the product—now "facial *cleaner*"—into something that would be more appropriately squirted onto your kitchen floor (which could use a good scrubbing, by the way) by a steam-spewing machine that you rented at the supermarket. But are we so impressionable that the tossing in of a little extra sibilance (real word!) is enough to upgrade a product from countertops to countenance? Why, yes. Yes, we are.

Clitoris, *noun*

The original "Like" button, a woman's clitoris is the most powerful trigger point for orgasm and is comparable to the flashing red launch button that's kept under a special flip-up plastic cover in many action movies. And, like that cinematic button, a short list of qualified individuals have unlimited access to it. Comprised of approximately 4.2 bajillion nerves, all of which go directly to the Happiest Place on Earth, the clitoris is not to be trifled with unless, of course, you happen to enjoy a good trifling. (Many ladies do.)

Closure, *noun*

A Zen-like state that is achieved once a breakup has been completely processed and every potentially romantic inclination you have toward your ex has been tracked and exterminated (*see also:* hatred and retribution). The last stop on the breakup journey, closure is marked by notably mild reactions to news about developments in the ex's life. For instance, post-closure responses to the revelation that your ex is seeing someone new might include, "That's nice," and "Good for him," in contrast to your recent pre-closure responses of performing four straight hours of Katy Perry karaoke on your apartment balcony and super-gluing a toilet seat onto the hood of your ex's truck.

Clothing Sizes, *noun*

Women's clothing sizes are assigned based on several different and arbitrary "systems." These systems may include the use of a dartboard, the firing of ping-pong balls across the designer's office into numbered buckets, or repeated flicking of a board-game spinner (*see also:* Twister). It's common knowledge that if you're a two at Banana Republic, you're a fourteen at Tory Burch. And yet . . . women find it virtually impossible to break free from the mental shackles of the size number. It vexes. It taunts. In retaliation, a woman is urged to disregard number sizes and give them no respect at all, but rather measure her attractiveness and self-worth against things that really matter, such as what kind of phone or car she owns.

Cocktail Ring, *noun*

First gaining popularity in the age of Prohibition, cocktail rings are typically dramatic in both size and design. Loaded with supersized style, the cocktail ring sends the message that its wearer knows a thing or two about a thing or two, including how to mix the perfect kir royale, which furrier in town can be trusted, and how to get the best-looking man in the room to light her cigarette without really trying. Available in a multitude of designs and price levels, the cocktail ring is one of those accessories that, regardless of price, will instantly have you trawling eBay for a cigarette holder and wondering where you left your vintage fox stole.

Color Analysis, *noun*

Also known as color seasons, this baffling system of skin and hair tone classification attempts to slot every woman into one of four color categories named for the four seasons and, by the way, is so complex that it would drive Albert Einstein to the crack pipe within five minutes. Warm? Cool? *What?* Geez, we just want to know if this lemon yellow T-shirt with the embellished teddy bear looks good on us or not, all right? Frankly, we are highly suspect of someone who pronounces that we are "a spring," and anyone who does so risks swift retaliation.

Combover, *noun*
A universally mocked and despised men's "hairstyle" that results when a man attempts to camouflage an area of baldness by growing his remaining hair to an extreme length and then plastering it across the thinning area. The result of this exercise is a repellent, unnatural effect that resembles a badly sodded lawn. The combover could be somewhat justified decades ago, but times have changed and baldness has been embraced as a perfectly acceptable and even preferable style choice among men throughout the sports and entertainment worlds. If this societal trend continues on its present course, researchers predict that the last combover in captivity will become extinct by the year 2025.

Comfort Food, *noun*
Any category of food or food item that you consume with the intent of improving your mood or outlook on life. People often turn to comfort food when they are facing an emotional challenge such as a breakup, family crisis, or professional setback. Although it is generally believed that male comfort foods are hearty and substantial (casseroles, steaks) and female comfort foods tend toward sweet snacks (ice cream, chocolate), compelling evidence exists that, given the right circumstances, no one would kick a bag of pork rinds out

of bed. There are also those who apply a more liberal definition of the term that embraces anything in the frickin' house, including last spring's Easter-basket dregs and earthquake/civil unrest supplies.

Commando, *adjective*

Most often used in the phrase "going commando," commando refers to the state of not wearing underwear. Most likely a derivative of various military terms that describe the practice of not wearing underwear under the uniform for the benefits of enhanced ventilation and reduced abrasion, enthusiasts claim the commando lifestyle to be superior in noncombat situations as well, citing, among other factors, a heightened sense of naughtiness. Additionally, going commando offers females the feature of completely eliminating any chance of the universally disparaged effect known as "visible panty lines" (*see also:* panty lines).

Condom, *noun*

Commonly known as a rubber, love glove, or world's tightest knee sock, the condom is an extremely popular form of birth control that performs several critical functions. First, the condom prevents pregnancy. Second, it helps prevent the spread of sexually transmitted diseases (STDs). Third, and perhaps most important, the use of a condom introduces the concept of the "mandatory time-out" into the lovemaking ritual, during which the man has the opportunity to show off his fumbling skills while serenading his waiting partner with erotic wrapper-ripping sounds. Also, some condoms come with little built-in speed bumps for your pleasure. You're welcome.

Continental Shelf, *noun*

The flesh platform created across a woman's chest when she has a spectacularly large bosom. Named for the edge of a continent that may or may not be underwater, this practical and nonderogatory term is used by females and is reserved for women whose chests are of a scale that presents specific wardrobe challenges. For instance, a particularly endowed woman might say while shopping, "I like this beach cover-up, but it does not adequately accommodate the continental shelf." For your information, under United Nations treaty, one's continental shelf is classified as territorial waters and will be defended as such.

Cottage Cheese, *noun*

1. A colloquialism for cellulite (*see also:* cellulite) that refers to the dimpled appearance caused by this reviled skin condition. **2.** A tasty, guilt-free food that can accompany most any meal and whose taste can be enhanced by pairing it with a variety of fruits or garnishes. Unfortunately, cottage cheese's image has been almost irretrievably sullied by its association with the dreaded skin condition of cellulite. As a result, some days it's all it can do to come out of its little plastic tub, even if the sun is shining.

Cougar, *noun*

The cougar is a woman, typically thirty-five and older, who actively seeks men twenty-five and younger as sexual partners. Famously noncommittal, the cougar enjoys the sport of sexual role-reversal, savoring her place as the huntress as she stalks her firm, young, and occasionally clueless prey in clubs, supermarkets, and sporting events. Intrinsic to the cougar concept is the notion that she is attractive, has taken excellent care of herself, is supremely confident and independent, and has become bored with her male peers and their baggage, ailments, and hang-ups. Elusive and strategic as her namesake, the cougar identifies her prey and strikes at her leisure. You do not find the cougar; the cougar finds you (or, more accurately, your hot brother).

Cougar Lift, *noun*
Plastic surgery undertaken by a woman specifically for the purposes of attracting younger men. This term is derived from the slang term "cougar" (*see also:* cougar), which refers to an attractive, middle-aged woman who is exclusively interested in pursuing younger men as sexual partners. The cougar takes excellent care of herself and is intent on retaining a youthful appearance . . . all over. When the time comes to incorporate plastic surgery into the maintenance regimen, she does so with an eye not toward the country club but toward the bedroom, selecting breast enhancement and buttock implants along with the typical facial fillers.

Couples Shower, *noun*
The couples shower can occur in connection with either an upcoming wedding or birth and is generally viewed as an attempt to "fold the men into the fun" no matter how vehemently the men try to convince the women that their idea of "fun" is not having to go to showers. The injection of male presence into the shower dynamic often takes the form of heckling, particularly during the gift-opening portion of the festivities. As the honored couple unwraps presents, male guests—especially those who are already married or have become parents—will attempt to enlighten their less-experienced

counterparts by shouting well-meaning warnings such as, "It's over, dude!" (wedding shower) or "Kiss sleep goodbye, chump!" (baby shower).

Coupon, *noun*
A highly effective marketing device that creates a powerful intersection of three concepts statistically proven to appeal to women: shopping (the motivation to purchase something), saving (the perception that said purchase exhibits financial shrewdness), and crafting (the activity of physically cutting out the coupon). Couponing can also activate a woman's organizational pleasure center through the use of a specialized (and, ideally, alphabetized) holder or sorter in which to tote the coupons to the store. The ritual of couponing is reinforced at the checkout stand when, if no coupons are presented in response to the request, the woman receives a small, shaming shake of the head and the silent reproach of the others in line behind her.

Couture, *noun*
This word is shorthand for the phrase "*haute couture*," which is French for "Who frickin' wears this stuff?" Famous for supreme drama and impracticality, a designer's couture collection is targeted to the extremely rarified demographic of women who barf money and can afford to hire people who will tell them that their $47,000 feather culottes look way better than those being worn by anyone else at the yacht club.

Crafts, *noun*
Any of a wide variety of typically homespun creative endeavors (quilting, macrame, pottery making, and needlepoint are just a few

examples), the prospect of which seems to have one of two distinct effects on most women: 1) they are drawn to the activity, curious about the required skills and supplies, and eager to express themselves through a new medium, or 2) they find the very notion of crafting and all that it implies repulsive and will remove themselves from the vicinity of a real or perceived crafts threat by any means necessary including sawing off their own arms.

Cramps, *noun*
Cramps are your body's way of saying, "Sisterhood, schmisterhood—I own your ass." Cramps can be described as a series of abdominal pains that range from a dull ache to the sensation of being repeatedly flayed with barbeque tongs, with accompanying levels of discomfort starting at "meh" and maxing out somewhere near "MOTHER AIYEOWOWOW!" Cramps can strike at any time prior to, during, or after your monthly period (*see also:* Aunt Flo, Festival of Menses). It is interesting to note that if you track your cramps and determine the monthly point at which the discomfort is greatest, you can be assured that your body will behave entirely differently the following month. Popular remedies for cramps include over-the-counter painkillers, application of a heating pad on your abdomen, and leaving work for the day so at least you don't have to have cramps *and* listen to your idiot boss.

Crimping Iron, *noun*
A specialized hair appliance that consists of two interlocking, wavy metal plates that are electrically heated to volcanic temperatures and then applied to a section of hair in a "munching" action that captures the hair between the plates and temporarily sears artificial

waves into it. Although many styling devices aim to create an effect that appears to have happened naturally, the crimping iron makes no apology for the decidedly unnatural result that comes from its use. It is safe to say that the tightly rippled and often Sphinx-like styles created through crimping iron use could be described as a "look."

Crows' Feet, *noun*
Any of the variety of crinkly, V-shaped creases that form around your eyes when you laugh or smile or, in later years, when you think or breathe. Named for the fact that the little lines give the appearance that a flock of birds just danced the Macarena across your face, crows' feet can be exceedingly difficult to eradicate once they've landed. Although topical creams such as Retin-A and mechanical processes such as microdermabrasion can help de-emphasize the appearance of crows' feet, many women feel that the best method for stopping these little birdies in their tracks is to immobilize the muscles underneath that allow the skin to crinkle (*see also:* Botox). Those uncomfortable with the concept of facial injections may undertake the mental conditioning required to rid one's face of all muscular emotional response, which, incidentally, also rids one's social calendar of all upcoming engagements.

Cujo Syndrome, *noun*
Named for the rabid St. Bernard in the popular movie based on Stephen King's novel of the same name, the Cujo syndrome describes the chronic affliction of having lipstick smeared across one's teeth. This unfortunate condition—with its accompanying startling appearance—happens to all lipstick-wearing women at one time or another, but we all know someone for whom it

seems to be a default setting. Why is this? Is it their brand of lipstick? Are they too aggressive in their application? Are they overly toothy? Under lippy? Do they not know the lipstick trick (*see also:* lipstick trick)? And what's the etiquette in this situation? Do we inform them that they appear to have just devoured a small animal or let them discover the gruesome truth for themselves when they glance in their rearview mirrors?

Culottes, *noun*

A word of French descent that stands for a skirt that has morphed into an awkward skirt/pants hybrid but is not a skort (*see also:* skort). Neither long nor short, neither pants nor skirt, culottes are, however, unwaveringly unattractive. Not to be confused with gaucho pants (*see also:* gaucho pants), that storied, swinging garment whose fierce, South American heritage is rekindled with every swirling mid-calf step, culottes stake out the anemic, knee-length middle ground and leave observers with the unsettling impression that the woman in question is, inexplicably, wearing a separate skirt on each leg.

Cunnilingus, *noun*

Fancy Roman word for oral sex involving the rhythmic, repetitive application of one's mouth and tongue against, into, onto, upon, around, about, and, if you're really motivated, *through* a woman's genitals. If performed with even a modicum of skill, cunnilingus will produce a typical reaction that falls somewhere between a grand mal seizure and being called up onstage at a Bon Jovi concert. Poorly executed cunnilingus, however, will result in a pitying tap on the provider's shoulder and an unsmiling, "Let's move on."

Curling Iron, *noun*

A hairstyling implement that includes a metal tube of varying diameter and an attached metal clamp, both of which, when plugged into an electrical outlet, become hotter than the earth's liquid-lava core. After the curling iron is heated (which should take anywhere from four seconds to thirty minutes), a section of hair is inserted into the clamp, wrapped around the barrel of the iron numerous times, and then flash-baked. Once ejected, the piece of hair releases a small puff of smoke and falls limply into its previous position where it loses its curl within five to seven minutes yet retains the asymmetrical bend-marks of the curling iron's metal shaft.

D

Daddy Issues, *noun*

A term of either disapproval or concern, commonly used in reference to a woman who is in a relationship with a man significantly older than herself. Although comments pertaining to daddy issues may sound surprisingly similar, the trained ear can distinguish the critical nuances in inflection that differentiate "Oh, dear, that poor girl is struggling with daddy issues," from "Man, does she have some daddy issues!" Even more difficult to discern is the additional category of comments that indicate an odd form of sibling rivalry in which a female onlooker will wonder why that daddy is not paying more attention to *her*.

Dame, *noun*

1. An archaic term for an adult female that, when used by a male, could be intended as either a neutral synonym for woman or a disparaging commentary on said woman. Popular beginning in the thirties, the word dame was often preceded by the phrase "high-class" and carried a connotation of civility that, in the galaxy of female labels, ranked it slightly higher than the coarser "broad."

Despite this, most women objected to this label, with the exception of, well, dames and broads. **2.** A fancy-pants British title for women that is the equivalent of knighthood.

Date, *noun*
1. A two-person social engagement that carries romantic overtones, although these can vary significantly among different couples as well as between the two members of the couple on said date (the latter type of which often explains the premature abandonment of a date). Date is a broad term that can encompass very loose and casual meet-ups as well as more formal outings that include a detailed grooming countdown, the presentation of small gifts or flowers, and elaborate car door-opening ceremonies. **2.** A commercial assignation with a professional sex worker, as referenced in the inquiry, "Hey, handsome, wanna date?"

Deflower, *verb*
A term for taking away a female's virginity (*see also:* virgin, precious flower). Deflower has a broad meaning that includes all aspects of the loss of virginity, including coarse and aggressive circumstances as well as more civilized encounters that feature deep-fried appetizers, an amusing romantic comedy at the local multiplex, and a chilled sixer of pretentious microbrew. It is theorized that the term's floral reference came about based on an observation that the undisturbed membrane of skin covering the entrance to the vagina (*see also:* hymen) resembles a flower. Interestingly, you never hear the surgical process of reconstituting the hymen (*see also:* revirginization) referred to as "reflowering."

Denim Rage, *noun*

Seething and/or outbursts of anger caused by wearing uncomfortably tight jeans. Statistics indicate that 94 percent of all denim rage-related incidents are caused by the so-called "denim denial effect," which occurs when a woman puts on her jeans in the morning, notes that they are uncomfortably tight, but decides to wear them anyway, convincing herself that they will become more comfortable as the day progresses even though she knows for a fact that the opposite trend will occur. Denim rage can strike at any time, but tends to be particularly severe after lunch. Denim rage is often mistaken for having a jackass for a boss, as both conditions provoke similar symptoms.

Dental Dam, *noun*

An incredibly sexy sheet of medical-grade latex that is plastered across your mouth and cheeks during oral surgery to isolate the target tooth or teeth while also preventing items such as dental instruments, cell phones, and eyeglasses from accidentally falling into your mouth during the procedure. But, wait, it gets sexier. The dental dam can also be used as a barrier during cunnilingus or analingus to protect against the transmission of STDs and, presumably, also help prevent items such as cell phones, eyeglasses, and party hats from falling into your . . . well, you get the picture.

Depilatory, *noun*

A term that evokes a harrowing surgical procedure or something really dirty that happens behind a closed bathroom door, a depilatory falls somewhere in between and is, in fact, a chemical solution that removes hair from the skin. Timing is key in using a depilatory;

if it is not left on long enough, the chemicals do not have adequate time to break down the hairs and the removal will be unsuccessful. In contrast, if the user becomes lulled by the old egg/dog vomit fragrance emitted by the depilatory solution and leaves it on the skin past the recommended time, it can cause redness and irritation, which most agree is pretty much as unattractive as the fuzz, especially if it occurs on the upper lip.

Dewy, *adjective*
The supposedly desired appearance of a woman's complexion. Although it is counterintuitive that you would want your face to look moist all the time, the word dewy is a popular one in cosmetics advertising. Do you want your skin to glow? Sure. How about freshness (*see also:* freshness)? Okay. The notion of walking around with one's face covered with a sheen of dew, however, simply takes it too far. Although we can make the connection, albeit a tenuous one, between the concepts of dew and youthfulness, we don't know a single woman whose goal it is to give her face the appearance of a ten-speed that's been left out in the yard all night.

Diet, *noun*
A rigid nutritional program designed with the intent of sucking every residue of joy from the process of taking sustenance into your body. Diets have been designed around virtually every aspect of humans and their foods, including blood types, sleep cycles, ethnicity, carb content, fat content, food color, food group, and the type of preparation applied to the food, if any. Whether the purpose of the diet is weight loss, weight maintenance, management of a health condition such as diabetes, or specialized preparation for an athletic

event, it can be said with certainty that Cheetos are not on the menu. Not that we're bitter or anything.

Dildo, *noun*

It's only a slight exaggeration to say that the dildo's defining characteristics are that it: 1) has been around forever, 2) is available in every material imaginable from mahogany to crystal to jelly rubber, 3) may light up, vibrate, or sing the national anthem, 4) is ideally shaped to slip cheerfully into any orifice that crosses its path, and 5) bears some sort of resemblance to a penis. Or not. Add to that the fact that the praises of this instrument of sexual pleasure have been sung in the works of Aristophanes, Shakespeare, and, more recently, the band Dildo Warheads, and you may conclude that, as humans continue to push outward in their exploration of space, the object that might best be left behind as a planetary calling card of the species is everyone's cylindrical (or not) friend: the dildo.

Diva, *noun*

Derived from the Italian word *diva*, meaning female deity, the term was originally applied to female opera singers of outstanding talent and notoriously high-maintenance personalities. As the decades passed, the term began to be applied more broadly to singers beyond the opera world (e.g., Diana Ross and Barbra Streisand) but retained its association with the notion of a demanding prima donna. In recent years, however, the diva label has moved out of its original rarified environment and into common usage with the emergence of such titles as "shoe diva" and "crafts diva," which we assume is someone who demands that a case of Evian and a crystal bowl filled with yellow M&Ms *only* be placed next to her sewing table.

Does This Make Me Look Fat?, *phrase*

A seemingly straightforward yet treacherous question that requires different responses depending on the gender of the person to whom it is addressed. When asked of a male, the reply must be a swift and emphatic, "No!" Ideally, this will be followed immediately with glowing modifiers such as, "You look hot!" and "Are you kidding? You need to *gain* a few pounds, hon!" When asked of a female, an honest response is acceptable, provided it is couched in camouflage comments that blame the unflattering appearance on the hateful designer, lousy dressing room lighting, and/or cheap construction of the offending garment.

Domestic Engineer, *noun*

The official term for a person (typically a female) who serves as facilities/plant manager of a domicile. This individual's areas of expertise include germ eradication, wardrobe maintenance, appliance repair, urban forestry, small animal husbandry, and culinary management. Depending on the particular household, the domestic engineer's responsibilities may also include preschool education, behavior modification, clinical psychological intervention, and anger management strategies. Studies have shown that the person ideally prepared for optimum service as a domestic engineer will have accrued extensive professional experience in the disciplines of electrical and structural engineering, crisis counseling, emergency medical services, community theater, and law enforcement.

Double Date, *noun*

A socio-romantic outing embarked upon by two pairs of people ostensibly for the purposes of maximizing the "fun," but often actually arranged in order to offer social support to more introverted couple members, to allow for team excursions to the ladies' room (*see also:* ladies' room) for exchange of vital information, or to give the more established of the couples an opportunity to model their adorable dating behaviors in a manner that encourages the "newbie" couple to emulate them. It is worth noting that although double dating provides a number of useful benefits, it also creates opportunities for so-called "comparison shopping," the results of which may not be in the best interests of all involved parties.

Douche, *noun*
1. A slang term, often lengthened to the more formal "douche bag," that describes an extremely self-obsessed male who acts like a jerk in order to appear cool. **2.** A feminine hygiene implement. In its archaic form, the douche was comprised of a rubber pouch and tubing that, left in your shower, gave your bathroom the ambiance of Frankenstein's lab. The modern, streamlined douche, however, comes in a box with pretty flowers on it and looks like something you'd find clipped to Lance Armstrong's racing bike.

Dressing Room, *noun*
A cramped pocket of space within whose bounds the laws of physics have no relevance. Known for its malfunctioning door latch, liberal scattering of straight pins, and ghoulish lighting, the dressing room can disorient even the most stable and secure of women, striking doubt into all who cross its threshold. The key component of the dressing room is its warped funhouse mirror, specially designed to inflate your dimensions from all angles while applying a sallow, rippling effect across every inch of exposed skin. Optional features

include a doorway curtain that is six inches too narrow to give you any privacy and a community three-way mirror in the dressing room hallway that encourages total strangers to weigh in on your clothing purchases.

Dude Biffle, *noun*
A variation of BFFL (best friend for life), the dude biffle is the male version of the female biffle. Filling the gap between the female friend and the GMF (*see also:* gay male friend), the dude biffle is someone who, regardless of attractiveness or availability, is never given romantic consideration but rather bypasses any sexual tensions and lands directly in the best friend category. The dude biffle is destined to remain a terminal nonromantic best friend unless you happen to be living in a romantic comedy, in which case you can expect there to be some kind of event that makes you suddenly look at him in a whole new light and wonder how you overlooked that you were in love with him, at which point he will announce that he's marrying your female biffle and high jinks follow to the accompaniment of a hit single–packed soundtrack.

E

Easy, *adjective*

The opposite of playing hard-to-get (*see also:* hard-to-get), easy takes up where overeager (*see also:* overeager) leaves off. This quaint term implies that a women does not have what might be regarded as the most rigorous screening process when it comes to selecting the recipients of her physical affections. On the contrary, the easy woman's policy might be more accurately described as "no one will be turned away." Charitable to a fault, this woman has a *modus operandi* that can, sadly, do considerable damage to her reputation over time. On the other hand, it just might get her a hit reality show, so who are we to judge?

Elevens, *noun*

Why do so many lousy things come in pairs? Uncomfortable shoes, mom jeans (*see also:* mom jeans), your annoying twin cousins, and now this: the two vertical creases between your eyebrows that have proven themselves impervious to the fifty-gallon drum of skin elixir you bought at the department store cosmetics counter. Plastic surgeons call them "elevens" because of their obvious resemblance to the number, but as far as you're concerned, those digits are 666. You're not sure when exactly they settled in, but you're certain you're not old enough to have those things and you know you don't scowl *that* much, so what the hell?

Elope, *verb*
To elope is to take a pass on the expense, time-consumption, and potential familial complications of a wedding and, instead, simply run away and tie the knot somewhere else, often without telling anyone you're going to do it. Although many people who have never been married can't imagine *not* experiencing the all trappings of a "real" wedding, it's safe to say that many married folks would— given the opportunity for a re-do—throw the suitcases in the car before you could say "Las Vegas." The notion of elopement also carries with it the sense that the wedding may be of a spontaneous nature or that there may be parties close to the couple who are very much against the union. As it can be difficult to convince people to spend thousands of dollars celebrating something they feel is the stupidest decision you've ever made, elopement often emerges as an ideal choice under these circumstances.

Engagement Ring, *noun*
The romantic, symbolic piece of jewelry that typically accompanies a marriage proposal and is donned by the bride-to-be upon her acceptance of said proposal. Most engagement rings feature a diamond solitaire, the most important qualities of which are color, cut, clarity, carat weight, and whether it's significantly better than all your friends' rings. Whereas the "four Cs" of diamond valuation have been attested to by gemologists and fall into clear-cut categories, the

friend-competition scale is more open to interpretation and ranges from, "Aw, what a sweet ring," (a one on the scale) to, "I never liked her anyway" (a resounding ten).

Espadrilles, *noun*
Shoes of French origin recognizable by their being assembled from canvas, rope, and other parts of a sailboat. Known for their formidable fantasy-inducing powers, espadrilles can transport even the most beaten-down Milwaukee office worker to a quaint Paris side street, where she finds herself doing something impossibly chic, like wearing the perfect white blouse while peddling a bicycle whose basket is full of those pointy bread loaves. Note: espadrilles should not be paired with a beret because, let's face it, a little French goes a long way.

Ethnic Joyride, *noun*
The practice of becoming involved with a man whose primary attraction—whether you realize it or not—is that he has a different ethnic or cultural background than you. For those who view life as a buffet, a day may come when you bypass your habitual, reliable Caesar salad and instead find yourself sticking your tongs into the bowl marked "Deviled Krab." Perhaps the last Caesar you had seemed a little routine, even with the additional scoop of croutons. Or perhaps this is the first time you've noticed the deviled krab's fluorescent sheen, its exotic texture, its essential un-Caesarness. What would it be like to be someone who goes for the deviled krab? And why have you gone this long without finding out?

Everyone Teased Me for Being So Skinny, *phrase*
One of two ubiquitous sound bites (*see also:* I was called ugly duckling in high school) regularly attributed to supermodels and sex-symbol actresses in order to make them sound more like average people. No doubt, this is a highly effective strategy and one that paints these women in a sympathetic light. After all, who would not be moved by the story of a young, aspiring spokesmodel who triumphs after years of being subjected by beastly classmates to scorching epithets such as "Leany" and "Slender-Face?"

Exfoliation, *noun*
Any procedure that mechanically scrubs or scrapes off dead skin cells, revealing supposedly "newer, fresher" skin underneath. There are many home methods of exfoliation, including granulated scrubs and creams, loofahs, pumice stones, and (*shudder*) metallic scraping devices. At the professional level, exfoliation can be a full sensory experience that includes sprinkles of sea salt or crushed nuts, mood-enhancing aromatic oils, and the haunting tones of the pan flute. It is worth noting that the physical experience of a thorough exfoliation can range from an invigorating buffing to the sensation of being pushed from a moving car onto the floor of the Mojave Desert.

Eyelash Curler, *noun*
A device that looks like it should be sitting on a sterilized tray in a lobotomy lab somewhere in Transylvania, but is actually an ingenious and only mildly terrifying tool found in most women's bathrooms or cosmetic bags. If done correctly, the process of curling one's eyelashes results in a pleasing "opening" of the eyes that can be quite dramatic. If done incorrectly, a different kind of drama

results—the kind that comes from neglecting to release the eyelashes before pulling the curler away from the face, at which point you panic and your hand clenches up, making it even more difficult to let go, and now your eyelid is way out in front of you like a patio awning and the very real possibility exists that your eyeball is going to dry up, which is a much bigger problem than having stick-straight eyelashes.

F

Face, *noun*

A shorthand term that stands for a woman's daily cleansing and cosmetic regimen that she undertakes before going out in public, often referred to as "putting on one's face." The components of this regimen vary significantly from woman to woman, depending on a number of factors including age, personal style, the manner in which she was raised, and the part of the country in which she lives. For instance, the "face" of a twenty-year-old woman living in Malibu might consist of nothing more than a quick cleansing and an application of sunscreen, whereas the "face" of a fifty-five-year old woman in Dallas might require sixty minutes, two dozen different products, and an airbrush machine. In short: your face, your rules.

Facelift, *noun*

A broad term that describes any surgical procedure whose goal is to give an overall "lift" or "freshening" to the face by counteracting the effects of gravity over time. As surgery methods have become more advanced, the process of a facelift has become less invasive, so that the term can now be used to include a facial rejuvenation done solely through injection—the so-called "liquid facelift." Regardless of the method, the end result of the facelift project—as with any other remodel—depends solely on the skill of the contractor you hire for the job. The downsides of an unsuccessful facial remodel can leave observers wondering if your perpetually startled expression is a result of the bill you received for the surgery or the realization that you don't look anything like yourself anymore.

Face Shapes, *noun*
Whether you like it or not, the shape of your face falls into one of several standard categories, which include oval, long, heart, round, and square. Some well-known examples of these shapes include Reese Witherspoon (heart), Charlie Brown (round), and Spongebob Squarepants (square). To determine the shape of your face, stand in front of a mirror, view your face, and ask yourself this question: "What shape is that?" Once you have identified your face shape, this information will influence many fashion decisions, such as hairstyle and earring choice. For example, if you have a "long" face, it's inadvisable that you cut your hair into a short bob unless your goal is to look like a thumb wearing a Willy Wonka wig.

Facial Mask, *noun*
Also available in extra-fancy "masque" form, the facial mask is a pasty substance that you smear on your face then allow to dry, creating a Freddy-Kruegeresque effect that is supposed to tighten the skin, shrink the pores, stave off breakouts, and generally improve your disposition. When the mask dries to the point that you feel your jawbone is about to wither and drop off your face, gently rinse it off.

Fun_fact_ If you've been waiting impatiently for a package to arrive, slip into your rattiest T-shirt, liberally apply the facial mask of your choice, then sit back and wait. Your doorbell _will_ ring.

Fake Bake, _noun_

Slang term for any kind of tan other than the one you get from actually being in the sun. Fake bake is most commonly used to refer to a faux tan that is aggressively unnatural looking, extreme (_see also:_ tanorexic), or poorly applied. Dead giveaways of the fake bake include streaked legs, "suntanned" heels, dingy finger webs, and stained cuticles. In addition, the fake bake is often accompanied by an unfortunate orange cast to the skin (_see also:_ whorange).

Fake It, _verb_

Pssst . . . can we let our hair down for a moment? There's no one else around, so it's safe to disclose the fact that sometimes—every now and then—a girl just needs some quality shuteye. That's not to say your man is anything but a fuel-injected love locomotive. But occasionally your sacred love rites might feel less like a little slice of heaven and more like you're being sawn in two by a very earnest magician. On these (rare!) occasions, most will agree that there's no shame in conjuring your inner amateur thespian and easing the way toward a blissful night's rest (as long as you remember to sell your performance all the way to the back row of the theater).

False Eyelashes, *noun*

These faux eyelash extenders come in a variety of forms and materials and can radically change the appearance of your eyes, giving them a lush, dramatic fringe. Not for the faint of heart or wobbly of hand, false eyelash application typically involves a package of eyelashes, tweezers, adhesive, and *a lot* of cussing. If you choose to apply individual eyelashes, expect to accidentally glue your eyelid shut two to four times. Using a single strip of lashes helps eliminate this problem, but increases your chances of looking down to find one of the strips nestled in your cleavage or clinging to an ice cube in your mojito.

Fashion Police, *noun*

The unfortunately fictitious squad of taste enforcers whose name is often invoked when witnessing an especially appalling style mishap (*see also:* fashion victim and "*Glamour* Don't"). Although it's unclear exactly what the bounds of the fashion police's jurisdiction would be, it's widely accepted that a legitimate and pressing need exists for this type of public service. Until the appropriate public policies are put into effect to allow direct intervention when fashion transgressions occur, society will have to rely on the existing websites, journalists, and bloggers who valiantly serve as whistleblowers on fashion's mean streets.

Fashion Victim, *noun*

We've all seen them, lounging in the mall food court or mingling among guests at a special event. Although they can be observed in many forms and at many price points, an everyday example of a contemporary fashion victim might be someone wearing jeggings paired with gladiator sandals, embellished tank top, military jacket, fedora, and chandelier earrings. (No, not you! You look *awesome*.) Like potato chips, trends can be impossible to resist when you've had just one (*see also:* trendster/trendwreck). Resist you must, however, or risk creating an unstable fad pileup that will have even the Hot Dog on a Stick Girls snickering behind your back.

Fat Pants, *noun*

Fat pants are the linchpin of every girl's wardrobe in that they perform a vital function called "keeping the dream alive." What dream is that? The dream that all that ice cream and beef jerky you ate last weekend liquified and dribbled out through your socks during Tuesday's four-minute treadmill "workout" rather than collecting in lumpy drifts between your belly button and knee caps. Fat pants are an instant pick-me-up when your regular jeans are annoyingly snug (*see also:* denim rage), allowing you to have a dialogue with yourself that goes something like this: "Hey, I thought I would have gained a couple of pounds from all the lasagna and chocolate mousse I ate at the company picnic, but check it out! These pants are *totally loose* on me!"

Fauxga, *noun*

A pernicious form of the centuries-old spiritual and physical practice of yoga that has been corrupted into a trendy, superficial workout fad. Particularly prevalent in "hip" urban centers, fauxga practitioners can readily be recognized by their sleek yoga outfits with coordinating accessories, the "Namaste" bumper stickers on their Range Rovers parked diagonally across two parking spaces, and the fact that they are the angriest-looking people barking into their iPhones while waiting in line at Starbucks.

Fellatio, *noun*
Although this sounds like the name of a stuffed puppet from some creepy kids' play in your neighborhood park, it's actually the official European name for oral sex performed on a man's penis (*see also:* blowjob). Although some women resist performing fellatio (*see also:* gag reflex), others enjoy it immensely and welcome most any opportunity to perfect their "moves." Note: fellatio is a legitimate term for this practice, however, it's not often used in casual conversation, so it's best not to refer to it as such or risk your boyfriend misunderstanding and thinking that he's finally convinced you to do that thing with the pliers and the nonstick spray.

Feminine Protection, *noun*
A term that describes the category of products designed and marketed to ease a woman through her monthly period (*see also:* Aunt Flo, Festival of Menses). Deceptively tough-sounding, feminine protection products are basically made from clouds of snow-white cotton, some with feather-light linings, covers, and even wings (coming soon: rainbows!). The "protection" portion of the phrase begs the question: protection from *what*, exactly? Society's unreasonable expectations? The harsh judgments of peers? The Man? Perhaps women seek refuge from Aunt Flo herself, who is so ruthless in her assault that at times only the most vigilant protection—yes, *overnight* protection—can hold her at bay.

Festival of Menses, *noun*

Menses is one of those medical words that at first you think must apply to some other species, like badgers, and then you find out that it *does* apply to you and you're stuck with it. So you try to spruce it up and make the best of it, hence the festival. The festival of your period, that is (*see also:* Aunt Flo). Are you fooling anyone with this? Not unless your goal is to throw a party that no one, repeat *no one*, wants to attend.

Figurine, *noun*

A figurine is a small statue, usually made of glass or china. No one knows when or where the practice of collecting figurines began, but the rituals associated with it appear not to have changed for centuries. In a nutshell, you buy a figurine, take it home, and place it alongside the others you have collected. For fun, you dust it, wonder how much you overpaid for it, and warn others not to do something stupid and knock it over. At some point, you begin using the word "valuable" to describe it, although others are overheard using words like "disturbing." Figurines are often passed down to younger generations as cherished keepsakes (*see also:* garage sale).

Fill, *noun*

The term that describes the process of getting your acrylic nails (*see also:* acrylic nails) partially reapplied by a nail professional. On average, a fill is performed every ten to fourteen days, the highlight of which is when the esthetician uses a small but lethal pair of nippers to pry any remotely loose portions of acrylic covering from the nails with an aggressive bending and digging action that often leaves the nail owners quivering and drenched in flop sweat. After prolonged negotiations, the client comes to an understanding with the esthetician that the final shape of the new acrylic nails should be "kind of oval but partially squared off, but not super-squared off, you know, because that's too harsh looking, so somewhere in between square and round and also not too long because last time they were a little too long . . . okay?"

First Date, *noun*

A highly anticipated social appointment for two people during which an extremely sophisticated system of mutual assessments is launched under the guise of "getting to know one another." Once the first date finally comes about, the pressure is on because both parties know that they are in the process of creating memories that will either be lovingly related to their children and grandchildren one day, or told between howls of laughter to their friends the following day (in which case the term "first date" becomes synonymous with "last date").

Fit Model, *noun*

This is the so-called "average-sized" woman on whom a clothing manufacturer will base a size in its line. This is an interesting concept, and one that conjures up a variety of images in consumers' minds as they attempt to find clothing they can actually wear. For instance, when you try on a piece of clothing at a store, you may inspect its fit on your seemingly average body and wonder where the manufacturer found a fit model with a trapezoidal torso, forty-inch arms, the complete absence of a butt, and a waistline that falls three inches below her nipples.

Flapjacks, *noun*

A playful, folksy nickname given by a woman to her breasts when, for one reason or another, they have experienced a loss of elasticity and/or fullness, leaving them with a silhouette that is reminiscent of the popular breakfast disc. The use of this term in reference to herself can exhibit a woman's healthy, realistic attitude with respect to the unreasonable expectations we often have about our physical appearances, as can be seen in the statement, "Hey, this dress makes my flapjacks look pretty good." Conversely, it can be an indicator of a festering dissatisfaction that may eventually lead the speaker to seek a surgical remedy to the situation, as exemplified by the statement, "What's the point of buying a cute bikini if these stupid flapjacks are just going to drag the top down to my navel?"

Flexting, *noun*

A contemporary mash-up of "flirting" and "texting" that gives everyone with a smidgen of technology at their disposal the ability (and courage) to send cute, intriguing messages to the objects of their affection . . . or at least their curiosity. As with all social interactions, flexting has a few ground rules. First, try not to be creepy; if your text could double as a line from a Wes Craven movie, keep it to yourself. Second, keep it clean, especially at first; no one wants to feel like she's just received her annual exam via AT&T. And last, accuracy counts. How'd you like to check your phone and find a message waiting that read *u nolg my harb fkank*?

Flirt, *verb*

To direct any of a multitude of behaviors toward another party that may or may not intend to convey the desire to have sexual intercourse with that party. Flirting with someone—either intentionally or accidentally—activates a complex, multifaceted concept that is plagued with vast differences in interpretation based on the gender of the person receiving said flirting action. For instance, most women will accept mild flirting such as a compliment or appreciative glance as nothing more than a fleeting ego boost, whereas many men on the receiving end of such actions interpret them as a sign from God that it's time to take off their pants.

Flirtationship, *noun*
A specific type of relationship that persists over time but exists solely on the flirtation level. You may have a flirtationship with your best friend's brother, a coworker, or the baristo with the nice forearms who makes your latte five mornings a week. In any case, the flirtationship has—at least in *your* mind—clear boundaries around it and, for whatever reasons, is destined never to progress beyond the flirting stage. Not to be confused with "friends with benefits" (*see also:* friends with benefits) the flirtationship could more accurately be termed "friends without benefits."

Flower Girl, *noun*
Female counterpart to the ring bearer, the flower girl is an excruciatingly adorable child whose task in the wedding ceremony is to do one or more of the following: 1) run screaming to her mother, father, or other approachable adult, 2) vehemently refuse to walk down the aisle under any circumstances, 3) jam her finger up her nose, 4) lie down, 5) make a loud, inappropriate announcement during exchange of vows (e.g., "I heard Grandma fart today!"), 6) scatter

flower petals along the way to the altar, creating an extra-romantic path upon which the bride may tread.

Food Porn, *noun*
Any of the current popular television shows devoted to the preparation, celebration, and consumption of food. Often presented in eye-popping, mouth-watering, high definition, food porn presents the entire food-preparation ritual in highly eroticized form, from the gentle washing of camera-ready vegetables to the vigorous whisking of a naughty hollandaise sauce to the tremulous shimmy of a gelatin mold when freed from the confines of its aluminum form. Whether your taste runs toward gentle titillation (down-home recipes in sweet country cottages) or you like it rough (international teams of chefs battling it out in sleek studio kitchens), you can be certain that, somewhere on the channel listings, there is a show for you. Just promise we won't walk in and find you basting.

Foreplay, *noun*
A rare and highly prized sexual practice in which the male primes the female for intercourse with a luxurious series of sensual treats, rather than simply pouncing on her and humping away like he's auditioning for a cameo on *Animal Planet*. Examples of mood-setting foreplay include such activities as erotic massage, "dirty" talk, and the joint consumption of sexy food in bed (brisket, for example). For married folks, these examples can be expanded to include such activities as getting the car smog-checked before the deadline and putting *both* socks in the hamper. Although foreplay exists in many forms depending on personal tastes, it is safe to say

that it does not include a nudge on the shoulder accompanied by the words, "You up?"

Foundation Garment, *noun*
The ominously named foundation garment comprises a category of women's intimate apparel that, although rarely referred to by this outdated name, remains the (feel free to sing along) *foundation* of a woman's wardrobe. Including all manner of bras, panties, and other under things, properly sized and designed foundation garments build a formidable superstructure that will suspend and present your clothing to the best possible effect. Besides, it's fun to say "foundation garment" just to mess with people's heads.

Freeway Face, *noun*
Slang term for the result of putting on one's makeup while piloting a vehicle. Hallmarks of freeway face include foundation streaks, jumpy eyeliner, lipstick on teeth (*see also:* Cujo syndrome), uneven blush (depending on which side of the car received the most sunshine), and, in extreme cases, small welts from a portable butane curling iron. In addition to the downgraded appearance resulting from slipshod cosmetic application, freeway face exacts a societal cost as well, as the distraction of applying makeup while driving leads to countless fender-benders as well as the senseless flipping of millions of innocent birds.

Freeway Penis, *noun*
A playful term used by a woman to describe the vehicle of a male whose sense of manliness clearly resides in said vehicle, which in turn casts serious doubt on the existence of any additional evidence

of manliness to be found on his person. Hallmarks of the freeway penis include exterior ornamentation such as after-market air dams and whale tails ("my penis has extra stuff on it"), eye-catching graphics ("my penis is flamin' hot"), the installation of devices that magnify engine sound ("my penis roars like a mighty cat"), and the purchase of so-called sports or "muscle" car models whose body designs resemble an actual penis ("my penis is really, um, penis-ish").

French Braid, *noun*
An intricate form of hair twining that leaves your locks snug against your head and, if done too aggressively, your brain thumping like a sub-woofer. The female population can be divided into two sub-groups: those who can French braid and those who can't. Although the French braid is recognized as an adorable hairstyle for little girls and adolescents, it is generally agreed that, among adults, it is worn to greatest effect by female law enforcement officers. Interestingly, despite its name, the French have repeatedly denied responsibility for the creation and/or popularization of this hairstyle.

French Tips, *noun*
A manicure technique in which the ends of the fingernails are painted white while the rest of the nail is glossed over with its natu-ral color. What is French about this? No one knows. It is suspected, however, that the people who created this name were hoping to pig-gyback on other super-cool things that start with "French," such as French kiss and French fries. In addition to the obvious upgrade in swankiness, "French tips" rolls off the tongue much more smoothly than "Uzbekistanian tips."

French Twist, *noun*

Here we go again with the fancy French stuff. The French twist is an excruciatingly chic hairdo that has been immortalized on some of the most beautiful and iconic women of the twentieth century. The French twist is created by twirling your hair up against the back of your head and tucking the ends inside, creating what the French refer to as "le wad." Next, jam approximately four thousand bobby pins into le wad while simultaneously emptying three cans of Aqua Net onto your head and cursing like a longshoreman. When your vision clears, use a hand mirror to view the back of your head (which should by now have the high-gloss sheen of a beetle's back) and admire your handiwork. *Voila!*

Frenemy, *noun*

The individual in your group of friends, likely female, whom you love to hate. Sure, you can tolerate splitting a cab to happy hour, but she always tries to outdo you by telling you about the new restaurant you *have* to try (but can't afford on your paycheck) or by posting 314 photos of her *ahmazing* trip to Fiji on Facebook. You secretly (or not so secretly) want to slug her . . . but you also kind of want to be her.

Freshness, *noun*

A mystical and highly desirable state that encompasses all things female. The quality of freshness should be apparent in your breath, your demeanor, your laundry, your scent, your hair, the new skin underneath the scaly layer you're making the rest of us look at, and your view of the world. Your approach should be fresh, along with your manicure/pedicure, and, if your makeup no longer looks fresh, then you should hightail it to the ladies' room and take care of that.

Inattention to the myriad aspects of female freshness can lead to a condition known as catastrophic freshness fail (*see also:* not-so-fresh feeling).

Friendly, *noun*

A person who may appear to be a member of your inner circle of friends, but in fact is not. One level higher than an acquaintance on the friend scale, the friendly may be someone from work, or perhaps a person you talk to each day at the gym, even the neighbor with whom you chat while walking your dog each evening. There is an invisible barrier between you, however, and whether she realizes it or not, the friendly's security clearance is restricted. She may know about the fight you just had with your boyfriend, but she doesn't know that you put his stupid Rams jersey in the donation box at the Salvation Army . . . because she's just a friendly.

Friends with Benefits, *noun*

A term that denotes a relationship between two friends that includes sex but does not involve the emotional involvement or commitment that traditionally accompanies a sexual relationship. A relatively recent concept that has emerged as the frontier of sexual freedom has been pushed further and further into the underbrush, the friends with benefits notion is not for the emotionally faint of heart. Rather, it requires the setting of manageable boundaries between two people who share an affectionate respect for one another, are mutually attracted on a physical level, and who have open, healthy channels of communication. As you can see, this is an entirely different dynamic than that of a boyfriend-girlfriend relationship.

Friend Zone, *noun*

A social categorization that corrals people whom you like but whom you do not consider to have romantic and/or sexual potential. Placement in the friend zone is accompanied by a "neutering" process that strips away any hormone-activating aspects of that person, leaving in their wake qualities such as "sweet," "fun," and the decidedly nonhot "nice." Placement in the friend zone is particularly frustrating to those who hope to generate a romantic connection because it is nearly impossible to upgrade one's status and regain sexual cachet after having been grouped with all those other sweet/nice people. What is the world coming to when people judge you to be kind and reliable without giving you a chance to show what a heartless, manipulative jerkwad you really are?

Fugly, *adjective*

Sometimes, when "ugly" just isn't going to get it done, you have no choice but to perform the linguistic version of stomping on the gas by welding the inflammatory "fuck" onto the front of the word. Mash them together and you've got the ideal blend of profanity and put-down: an insult perfect storm. Although fugly carries an obvious negative connotation, in the future you can expect this pattern of word creation to spawn more positive words as well, including "funusual," "fincredible," and "fawesome."

G

Gag Reflex noun
1. A totally legitimate condition in which the back of the throat is so sensitive to sensation that even the slightest stimulation evokes an immediate gagging response in an effort to eject the offending item causing said stimulation. **2.** A made-up and highly effective excuse that is sometimes claimed by a woman who is, for one reason or another, not terribly motivated to perform oral sex on a male or who is ready to segue out of an oral sex session already in progress due to uncomfortably aggressive ramming by the male. Note: the effectiveness of this term can be exponentially increased when paired with the term "lockjaw."

Garter, *noun*
An embellished elasticized band worn on the thigh by a bride. The garter is typically made of satin or silk and lace and often is light blue in color, satisfying the "something blue" portion of the wedding tradition as well as the "something slutty" practice that has gained popularity in recent years. At the wedding reception, the groom removes the bride's garter to great fanfare and the wedding-band

version of "The Stripper," then flicks it into the crowd of male onlookers to a chorus of "You're next, Dude!" The garter then hangs from the rearview mirror of the recipient's Honda where it will be a badge of honor in the mall parking lot for years to come.

Gauche, *adjective*
Like "chic," this is one of those words that automatically locks up your jaw and makes you feel superior to everyone else in the room. Also like "chic," you're not sure exactly what qualifies for this label, you just know it's a really classy slam. A close cousin to "tacky," gauche seems to be the put-down of choice for something that has an inherent air of upper crust about it. For instance, you might say that your great aunt's wearing of her heirloom diamond brooch on her bathrobe was *gauche*, whereas her wearing said bathrobe to the liquor store was *tacky*. See the difference?

Gaucho Pants, *noun*
Also known simply as gauchos, gaucho pants are inspired by and named for the wide, cropped pants typically worn by traditional South American "cowboys" or *vaqueros*. Most often made from stretchy, flowing fabric, gaucho pants have the swirl and panache that's missing from their tight-lipped cousins the culottes (*see also:* culottes). Unfortunately, gaucho pants present a serious footwear dilemma when removed from the pampas and placed into an urban context; they are too casual to wear with dressy shoes, casual shoes make them look like cut-off sweatpants, and, if you wear boots with them you end up looking like an extra from one of the *Pirates of the Caribbean* movies.

Gay Male Friend, *noun*

The gay male friend (GMF) is a near-perfect nonromantic companion for today's female. Taking up where typical female friendships leave off, the GMF relationship injects a masculine point of view into the mix while avoiding much of the stereotypical stealth competitiveness that can torpedo some female friendships. That's not to say that GMF relationships are perfect, or even superior, but rather a uniquely delightful component of a fortunate woman's inner social circle. As many women will attest, when life poses those tough questions, it's often the GMF who can be relied upon to provide the, um, straightest answer.

George Glass, *proper noun*

Originally invented by Jan on *The Brady Bunch* after "Marcia, Marcia, Marcia" won yet another boy's heart, George Glass is now the generic term for an imaginary boyfriend. Most often invoked in an effort to hide the fact that you are single or currently sleeping with someone else's husband, your George Glass will likely have a (lucrative!) career that keeps him traveling at least two-thirds of every month, although he'd obviously rather be home with you. An advanced imaginary-boyfriend enthusiast will occasionally break up with her George Glass just to make sure he doesn't start taking her for granted.

Giant Sunglasses, *noun*

Popular among celebrities and mortals alike, oversized sunglasses are available in three diameters: 1) coaster, 2) flower pot, and 3) cruise ship porthole. Arguably the next best thing to put on your face if you have to run out to the store without your makeup and you don't happen to have the windshield of a 747 handy. Paradoxically, giant sunglasses serve to obscure the identity of the wearer while simultaneously screaming, "Hey, get a load of me! I'm wearing big-ass sunglasses!" In addition to hiding the evidence of last night's unfortunate absorption of an entire cluster of Worcestershire-Tequila Skull Scourers, giant sunglasses apparently also protect your eyes from something called "the sun's harmful rays."

Gift with Purchase, *noun*
A magical retail term that arouses passion in even the most miserly of females. It is estimated that approximately $38 billion is spent each year by women attempting to meet the minimum purchase requirement and qualify for a "free" faux-vinyl cosmetic bag filled with a sample of eyebrow-firming elixir, a tube of forest green mascara, and a two-ounce bottle of Sex Me Up Wild Artichoke eau de toilette with a malfunctioning sprayer. (*See also:* while supplies last!)

Girl Friday, *noun*
An archaic term used almost exclusively by a male to describe a female assistant. Derived from the name of the character in *Robinson Crusoe* who was rescued from cannibalistic sacrifice to become the protagonist's unquestioning manservant for the rest of his days, the term girl Friday was once quite common in the business world and conveyed the idea that the woman in question was skilled at performing almost any task requested of her and therefore indispensable. Over time, however, the girls of Friday—along with those of the other workdays—began to feel that success in a position named for a captive servant was much less likely than it was for their male

counterparts who were given clever nicknames such as "manager" and "account executive."

Girdle, *noun*

Your grandmother probably wore one, and your great-grandmother certainly did, but as a modern woman, you have other, more advanced options for figure control (*see also*: Spanx). The girdle is an old-fashioned undergarment that was once the staple of a grown woman's underwear arsenal (*see also:* foundation garment). Unyielding and extremely structured, the traditional girdle came in a range of forms, from a simple steel-belted panty to an hourglass-enforcing device of continental proportions.

Girl Scout Cookies, *noun*

The SCUD missile of dessert items, Girl Scout cookies can blast through the most impenetrable of diets and make rubble of ironclad New Year's resolutions faster than you can say "I'll take four boxes of Samoas." What *is* it about these things? You know if they were on the supermarket shelves, you'd walk right past them without a second look, right? Is it their limited-time availability? The fact that you get hit up for them at the office when you'd rather do anything but finish writing that report? Is it the smiles of little girls whose hopes and dreams have not yet been crushed under the boulder of life's realities? More importantly, *is anyone selling them here today, right now?* We've got CASH, people!

Girly-Girl, *noun, adjective*

This term has many shades, all of them pink. The girly-girl is a self-proclaimed enthusiast of all things feminine—the rufflier the better.

As such, she adheres to strict, traditional gender roles and can often be found sitting in a car, waiting for a man to come around and open the door for her. In its use as an adjective, the term girly-girl can carry a positive, neutral, or negative connotation. For instance, if you are up at bat in a softball game and someone on the field yells out "girly-girl batter," you have been disparaged and should retaliate by smoking the crap out of the ball and clearing the back fence.

Give Up, *verb*

We've all been there—when all the upkeep, the grooming, the exercising, *all* of it, just feels so futile, so pointless (*see also:* throwing in the towel, hanging it up). It's hard not to have these days every once in a while, especially when your hormones have gone rogue and you are getting a beat-down from Aunt Flo. The good news is that everyone feels this way sometimes, no matter how fabulous they may appear to be. You know, for instance, that even Lady Gaga looks in the bathroom mirror sometimes and thinks, *Geez, what a project. Tonight I'm just going to stay in, wear my fat pants, and watch* The Bodyguard.

Gladiator Sandals, *noun*

Another item in the realm of combative footwear for women (*see also:* over-the-knee boots), gladiator sandals are the perfect choice for the woman who tries on a pair of regular sandals, looks in the mirror, and says to the salesclerk, "These are cute, but do you have anything bloodthirstier?" Constructed of multiple leather straps that, on some styles, reach all the way to the knee, the gladiator sandal sends the message that, in addition to gum, tissues, and car keys, an inventory of the wearer's handbag will also yield a trident.

Glamazon, *noun*

A term formed from the combination of "Amazon" and "glamour" and used to describe a woman who is typically large in stature, extremely devoted to fashion, and potentially warlike. Borrowing from the fierce, threatening nature of history's Amazon women—those bands of female warriors who routinely suited up to whup male heinie on any number of battlefields—today's glamazon stalks the earth unapologetically, her very beauty and fashion savvy striking fear into all who behold her.

Goddess, *noun*

A benevolent female title applied to oneself or bestowed by others that indicates exceptional powers or tendencies in a particular capacity. Although often confused with diva or maven, goddess conveys neither the high-maintenance behaviors of the diva (*see also:* diva) nor the strategic social influence of the maven (*see also:* maven). Rather, the goddess seeks to shed loving, helpful light on those around her, who are in turn awed by her gracious selflessness. For example, if you were taking a sewing class and ran out of thread, the diva would claim she had none to spare, the maven would explain what type of thread you should buy and why, and the goddess would give you all of her thread and maybe even rub your feet.

Granny Panties, *noun*

The wearable version of comfort food (*see also:* comfort food), granny panties are like an intimate hug from an old, asexual friend. After a day in the grating clutches of a lace thong, or even the less constricting but potentially wandering hipster, there are few garments as understanding—as deeply *accepting*—as the granny panty. There is no judgment in these drawers, not a whiff of reproach. There is only the safe, snug harbor that awaits in your dresser drawer each day, ready to welcome you once again into its voluminous folds where it will caress you as always with its cotton or cotton-nylon-blend embrace.

Greige, *adjective*
A portmanteau of "gray" and "beige" that forms the name of the color created when these two shades are combined. Recently rotated to the top of the trendy-colors list, greige has become the "hot" shade for nails as well as interior design, making it difficult to flip through a fashion or home magazine without encountering this impossible-to-nail-down color on fingertips and/or walls. Is it gray? Is it beige? Does it compliment *any* skin tone? And what's next on the color-combo horizon? Grellow? Blorange?

Gunne Sax, *noun*
A retro brand of cotton formal dresses that peaked in popularity in the seventies. At the time, the typically multitiered, printed Gunne Sax formal was the height of fashion for tween and teen girls attending school dances and other special occasions that called for their faux-prairie finest. To utter the phrase "Gunne Sax" is to evoke an entire fashion vibe that included feathered hair (or at least you tried to make it feather), clunky wooden platforms, a fringed suede purse, Bonne Bell lip gloss, and a generous spritzing of either Love's Baby Soft or Charlie! Next stop: Funky Town.

Gym Membership, *noun*

A key component of the long and rewarding process of pretending to commit to a fitness regimen. Each and every day, millions of people tour their local health clubs where they scrutinize locker room facilities, ask penetrating questions about elliptical-machine availability, and somberly observe spin classes like diplomats touring a developing nation. Time-consuming as it is, this is a crucial step toward selecting the gym you will avoid going to for months—or even years (*see also:* New Year's resolutions). Once a member, you'll begin to enjoy the benefits of seeing your monthly membership charge on your credit card statement and, seasons later when you've forgotten exactly where that gym is, you'll still feel a buzz of pride and think, *Damn, I'm glad I joined that gym.*

Gynie, *noun*

A cute but grating nickname for your gynecologist. There seem to be two schools of thought on how to interact with one's gynecologist. The first involves a casual, folksy approach with the goal of making the exam as unintimidating as possible. Common strategies include leaving a complimentary soy latte by the sink in the exam room, inviting your doctor to be your Facebook friend, and addressing him or her as "Chief," "Sport," or "Doctor Awesome." The second approach is more formal and dictates that you direct all medical questions to the receptionist (when she's off the phone with her boyfriend), keep your eyes respectfully on the ceiling for the duration of the appointment, and, if you must speak directly to your doctor, address him or her as "Your Excellency."

H

Handbag, *noun*

Also commonly known as a purse, a woman's handbag is a microcosm of her lifestyle, serving both as a receptacle for the items she requires while on the go and as a communicator of her style identity to the world at large. As such, the selection of a handbag is a delicate and complex one that must take function, fashion, and price point into consideration. Many males approach a woman's purse with extreme wariness, and rightly so. To root through a woman's purse is to explore her very psyche. This is a journey that most men, given the choice, would rather skip than risk encountering something that might give them pause, be it a pacifier, a litter of maxi pads, or a Saturday night special.

Happy Trail, *noun*

Unlike the dusty path into cowboy sunset of which Roy Rogers sang, this brand of happy trail can be found on many men's torsos (and we're guessing that most of them would rather you not tread on it with your horse). The happy trail, also known as the treasure trail, is the path of hair that starts anywhere in the mid-tummy area and extends down past the belly button until it eventually merges with the pubic hair. Hikers should be aware that there can be great variances in terrain among happy trails that can include shifts in vegetation from sparse to dense, sudden changes in incline of the trail, and unexpected increases in humidity.

Hard-to-Get, *adjective*

How you're supposed to play. The opposite of overeager (*see also:* overeager), playing hard-to-get is, according to conventional wisdom, the way to pique a man's interest in you. This strategy works because men love something called "the chase," and if you make their pursuit of you too easy, well, that takes the fun out of it. (Hey, we don't make the rules—we're just passing them along.)

Fun*fact* It's possible to play the hard-to-get game a little too well (see also: eye gouge), which can result in the man's confidence being irreparably crushed, at which point he will think you're just plain mean.

Harem Pants, *noun*

Putting the traditional dress of various geographic and ethnic groups aside, harem pants refers to the contemporary version of this skirt-that-thinks-it's-pants garment. Worn most notably—and to great effect—in recent decades by musician MC Hammer (who launched the term "Hammer pants" into popular vernacular), harem pants proved themselves to be perhaps the most unrestricting yet eye-catching dancewear since the birthday suit. Though only a fool would call the Hammer's pants judgment into question, the success of harem pants as an appealing item of clothing on the average male or female remains a subject of heated debate.

Hatred and Retribution, *noun*

A crucial period following a breakup in which you move from a place of wounded mourning into a bitter yet therapeutic place of realizing your ex is an asshead crapweasel. The hatred and retribution phase is marked by a spectrum of behaviors including, but not limited to: 1) defacing photographs, 2) squinting off into the distance while shaking your head and snarling, and 3) posting your ex's phone number in various anti-U.S. rant forums known to be under surveillance by Homeland Security. It's worth noting that you cannot reach the magical state of "closure" without passing through hatred and retribution and, although you'd like to think of yourself as someone who's above that sort of thing, we both know that's not the case.

Hawt, *adjective*

An affected spelling and pronunciation of the word "hot" associated with teens and tweens as well as those of more advanced age who would like to be identified with youth culture. A popular term in texting, hawt is used to indicate extreme hotness, also described as attractiveness. It is worth noting that, with the appropriate sneering delivery, hawt can take on an opposite meaning and become a term of derision, as in, "Oh, my, look at Krysta's new mom jeans. *Hawt.*"

Headache, *noun*

Undoubtedly one of the most versatile and effective of the potentially fake maladies, the headache has been a friend to womankind for thousands, wait, make that *millions* of years. (It may not have been discovered yet, but somewhere in the world there exists a cave painting that depicts a frowning woman wearing a bear skin and gesturing at her head while a dejected-looking man points longingly at their Stone Age sofa bed.) The truth is that sometimes women, just like men, simply aren't into it. (Okay, this may be the case *slightly* more often for women than for men.) On these occasions, a woman may feel that pleading a headache is gentler on her partner's feelings than saying that she's not in the mood.

Fun*fact* Some women's headaches are actually real.

Headband, *noun*
Not to be confused with either the decorative accessory or the functional, sweat-absorbing counterpart worn on the forehead, the headband is a rigid, U-shaped implement that rides across the top of the head with the purpose of holding the hair away from the face. In addition to this practical use, the headband ostensibly serves a decorative, fashion function as well, although no reliable evidence exists to support this theory. Available in a spectacular selection of colors, widths, and materials, the much-maligned but hardworking headband took what may have been a terminal image hit when Hillary Clinton made bulky, fabric-covered headbands her signature hair accessory, unleashing from the formerly docile headband-haters a torrent of criticism that continues to this day.

High Tea, *noun*

Also known in the abbreviated form of simply "tea," this is a traditional female get-together at a hotel or tea room during which women drink various blends of tea, consume miniature sandwiches and/or scones, and exchange tidbits of polite conversation while pretending that 1) they do this crap all the time, and 2) they're not the one who just valeted the Hyundai with the kitty litter spilled all over the driver's seat. High tea is one of those occasions when you can get your *My Fair Lady* on (*see also:* pinky) by wearing something feminine and demure, sitting up straight, and doing your best not to use words that include the suffix "-sucker."

High-Waisted Jeans, *noun*

A vintage style of denim pants that existed for centuries before the perfection of modern waist-lowering technology, thus freeing women from jeans that made their bottoms look as tall as Trump Tower. Although popular culture has embraced low-waisted jeans, which have stayed in fashion since their introduction, there remain pockets of women across the United States who have rejected the low-waist trend, apparently preferring the lifestyle that comes with a fourteen-inch fly and belt loops that are so high on the torso they can double as a push-up bra.

Himbo, *noun*

Slang term for a male who is judged to be, as the expression goes, "easy on the eyes," but falls considerably (okay, epically) short of being an intellectual powerhouse. A rogue masculine form of the word "bimbo," both himbo and its female counterpart are lousy, stinkin' stereotypes based on physical appearance and, as such, we are officially appalled that you would even consider including them in your vocabulary. If, however, you are basing your categorization on significant firsthand experience that includes multiple, unsuccessful attempts at meaningful conversation with the male in question, well, then just sit back and enjoy the view as your himbo tries to explain what happened on the last episode of *Jersey Shore*.

Hipster, *noun*
The very essence of in-between-ness, the hipster is neither thong nor granny panty, but rather something . . . in the middle. Will it give you panty lines? It might and it might not. Does it poke out above the tops of your jeans? Depends on just how low-cut your jeans are. Is there a significant likelihood of wedgie with the hipster? Hard to say. There could be, but then again, you might be all right on that. Are you commitment-phobic? The hipster may very well be your drawers Nirvana.

Hitler 'Stache, *noun*
An unfortunately named pubic topiary design that consists of a small, neatly groomed square or rectangle of hair on the mons. Not to be confused with the landing strip, the Hitler 'stache looks more like your landing strip has been cut short and you'd be lucky to set a helicopter down on that tiny patch of turf. Named for its resemblance to the icky little mustache favored by the infamous twentieth-century dictator and sociopath, this may be the waxing style most in need of an image makeover. As small as the 'stache may be, it still provides a last outpost of hair, canceling out the prepubescent girl/shaved cat comparisons that can be troubling to both men and women.

Honeymoon, *noun*

The term for the vacation that a newlywed couple takes immediately following their wedding, honeymoon has a number of charming historical origins that no one cares about. What we *do* care about is that your mother stayed sober through almost the entire ceremony, no one seemed to notice that the flowers on the cake were brown, the maid of honor promised not to post the photos from the bachelorette party on Facebook, and everyone seemed to buy the story that your tux pants were six inches too short because it was Tom Ford's new "Capri tux." Damn, we need a vacation.

Hoo Haa, *noun*

This term, with its various spellings, holds the distinction of being by far the most jubilant of the euphemisms coined for female genitalia. In fact, enthusiastic delivery of this term is sometimes enough on its own to incite a spontaneous orgy (or rodeo, depending). Generally regarded as a nonderogatory term, hoo haa is frequently used by women seeking a cute, generalized shorthand that can be spoken in polite company when the discussion turns to, um, one's genitals.

Hormones, *noun*

Your body's natural angel dust, hormones call the shots whether you want to admit it or not. They run your biological clock, mess with your complexion, inflate your butt, hang up on your boyfriend, and drive your car to the hatchet store with you in it.

Hot Flash, *noun*

A delightful and exciting side effect of menopause (*see also:* menopause) and/or perimenopause (don't ask) that involves a sudden, extreme increase in body temperature that lasts, on average, anywhere from two to thirty minutes. Side effects of the hot flash can include the rapid appearance of a significant amount of perspiration, heart palpitations, and reddish flushing of the skin (spawning the corollary term "hot flush"). Women who exhibit these symptoms exclusively while sleeping get to use the even less appealing term "night sweats" to describe the experience. Nonmedical side effects of hot flashes can include swearing, repetitive showering, heightened dry-cleaning expenditures, and general bitterness.

Hot Glue Gun, *noun*

Crafts weapon of choice for millions of women (and approximately two dozen men), the hot glue gun is one of the most reliable and versatile tools to be found in your home (*see also:* vibrator). Effective at securing everything from the sequins on your baton to the trim on your hatchback, glue guns come in many models and sizes to suit your particular needs. Although many women view crafts with extreme suspicion and/or derision and swear up and down that they would never even consider owning a hot glue gun, scientists predict that by March 28, 2019, you will have one whether you want it or not. Yes, eventually the hot glue gun—like the rhythm—is gonna get you.

Hot Mess, *noun*

A term that is used when it's simply not enough to say that someone is a mess, and a modifier is necessary to indicate that the mess in question has been heated to a temperature sufficient to make it critical. The hot mess is in crisis on all fronts simultaneously and this fact is evident even to the most casual observer. Hallmarks of the hot mess can include, but are in no way even remotely limited to: 1) tear-streaked face (with or without streaming mascara), 2) wringing hands, 3) loud and/or shrill voice, 4) full-body agitation, and 5) repetitive asking of questions that have no sane answers.

Hymen, *noun*

Also known as the "flap heard 'round the world," the hymen is the thin membrane of skin that can be found—or not—across the opening of a female's vagina. For a large portion of human history, the presence of an intact hymen has been used as evidence of virginity (*see also:* virgin, revirginization). The truth of the matter, however, is that this in an entirely inaccurate method as the hymen is extremely delicate and can be torn or dislodged through a variety of nonsexual activities such as vigorous interpretive dance, camel-racing, or even, let's face it, a really good sneeze.

Hyperdating, *noun*

The contemporary practice of dating a large number of people in a short period of time in order to accelerate the process of finding a long-term mate. Serious hyperdaters can find themselves going on seven or more first dates per week as they rapidly cycle through their local inventory of available partners while streamlining their personal checklist of compatibility requirements. Note: although the terms sound similar, hyperdating is not to be confused with speed dating, which involves a furious, round-robin style pitchfest during which participants are given only moments to sell the stranger across from them on the merits of their [*ding!*]—we're sorry, we're out of time for this definition, but here's our number because we think you're really cute.

I

I Hate You, *phrase*

This is one of those expressions that is, as they say, all in the delivery. If spoken in a menacing or even straightforward manner, its meaning is, well, pretty clear. If, on the other hand, it's exclaimed by one female to another with a seemingly warm or jovial inflection, it becomes a complex expression of admiration and/or envy. An example of this more subtle use of the phrase might be: "Omigod, that dress makes you look so skinny! I hate you!" It's important to realize that when someone uses this expression with you she actually does, in some small way, hate you.

Implant Impalement, *noun*

The unintentional discomfort inflicted when receiving an especially boisterous hug from a woman who has breast implants and who has not made adjustments in her hugging style that take the new firmness of her chest into account. An increasingly common occurrence in today's society, the severity of implant impalement can be ranked on a pain scale from A to DD, though some argue that the degree of distress is not correlated to cup size. Although almost everyone appreciates a good, solid hug, incidents of implant impalement are spurring the creation of new, defensive hugging maneuvers such as the Arm's Length, the Do-Si-Do, and the Left-Right Fake.

Impotence, *noun*

The physical inability of a man to achieve an erection sufficient for sexual intercourse (*see also:* it happens to everyone). Impotence can strike a man anytime, but it's widely agreed that pretty much the worst time is when that man is trying to have sex. With you. Yes, that's definitely the worst time. Anyway, men are super sensitive about this condition, which means you are going to have to tap dance your little heart out to convince him it's not a big deal and he is still every bit the strapping test pilot/lumberjack/cowboy you've always thought he was. In addition to the touchstone "It happens to everyone," other useful phrases you can whip out (don't say "whip out," btw) include "You're too much for me anyway" and "I just love cuddling."

Internet Spouse, *noun*

A nickname for the person you spend the most time connecting with on the Internet, either directly through e-mail, or via social media such as Facebook and Twitter. More than just a casual web friend, your Internet spouse is someone with whom you have robust daily contact that is second only to your daily communications with your IRL (in real life) partner or spouse. Whether or not it carries romantic overtones, this category of relationship offers a number of advantages, including a minimal personal hygiene requirement, never having to pretend to fight for the check, and the ability to claim ISP difficulties if you don't feel like talking with him.

Investment Piece, *noun*

If you're like most people, this phrase scares the crap out of you. As it should. Traditionally, investments are supposed to be things like real estate, not some iconic handbag that is likely to be splattered with Jamba Juice three days after you get your hands on it. It sure sounds nice, though, doesn't it? "Oh, this? Yes, this is my new raincoat. It's an investment piece, you know. See the plaid lining? It cost *bank*. Yes, I know it's sunny today. You don't think I'm going to wear this thing in the *rain*, do you?"

-ista, *suffix*

A very handy feminine suffix that can be attached to almost any noun with the effect of amplifying its meaning beyond its original proportions while also implying an additional level of fierceness. The presence of -ista reminds the reader/listener that the noun in question is a force to be reckoned with and is prepared to take you down at the first hint of disrespect. Think about it for a moment: would you rather list your home with a realtor . . . or a *realtorista?*

It Bag, *noun*

This term was coined in the nineties when designers realized that the sport of competitive purse-carrying was spreading from the realm of the wealthy and into the ranks of the everyday shopper willing to plunk down the equivalent of a mortgage payment or more for the privilege of toting the fetish accessory of the moment. Exemplified by such models as the Louis Vuitton Speedy, Hermes Birkin, and Fendi Spy, the it bag craze has largely gone underground in the wake of recent, large-scale economic challenges and resulting New Austerity, which dictates that it's currently cool to show one's support for those folks facing hard times by pretending to carry "regular" handbags.

It Happens to Everyone, *phrase*
One of two essential phrases that every woman must know (*see also:* size doesn't matter), "It happens to everyone" has been credited with salvaging many an evening, not to mention entire marriages. Although this phrase is usually effective in soothing your man's ego should impotence rear its ugly head (sorry, bad choice of words), there may be times when you need to assuage his feelings of inadequacy by blaming external factors for the unfortunate turn of events. These might include a sudden change in atmospheric pressure, the constant snarling of your roommate's dachshund outside your bedroom door, or recent sunspot activity. Note: when using this phrase, it's important *not* to give the impression that you have firsthand knowledge of it happening to "everyone," because, trust us, that's not going to help the situation at all.

It's Not You, It's Me, *phrase*
This mammoth whopper is the bedrock of the entire breakup system as we know it. As ridiculous a notion as it is that someone would break up with his partner because of dissatisfaction with *himself,* this chestnut continues to be called up when the person doing the breaking is trying to spare the feelings of the person being broken—a noble intention, but *come on.* (Of course, if your boyfriend recently broke up with *you* and said "It's not you, it's me," well, that's an obvious exception to the above and we're sure he *totally* meant it. You are so much better off without him and also we really like your

new perm.) Anyway, just so we're clear, it is always, *always* you. It is *never* me.

IUD, *acronym*

Acronym for intrauterine device (not, as commonly believed, "in up 'dere"), the IUD is a form of contraception that involves planting a piece of plastic that looks like one of those floss-picker things into your uterus, where it floats around like Sputnik until your gynecologist (*see also:* gynie) removes it. Although the IUD produces several effects that work to prevent conception, its general method is to irritate and eventually piss off your uterus so much that it shuts the blinds, changes its phone number, blocks you on Facebook, and refuses to play nice with any of your partner's sperm until the annoying device is removed.

I Was Called Ugly Duckling in High School, *phrase*

One of two standard quotes (*see also:* everyone teased me for being so skinny) regularly attributed to supermodels and sexpot actresses in an effort to make them sound more like regular ol' folks. We're sorry, were those hard times? Do those old taunts come back to haunt you when you're on the sun deck of your yacht running barefoot through Jake Gyllenhaal's chest hair? Listen, some of us were called things like Scrotum Wind and The Turdinator—and that was just kindergarten. All *we* have now to ease the pain of those memories is a boyfriend who's "keeping his options open" and a Camry whose driver-side window only shuts halfway.

"I Will Survive," *song title*

This female-power masterpiece, written by Freddie Perren and Dino Fekaris and performed by Gloria Gaynor, is arguably the ultimate post-breakup recovery song (*see also:* breakup). Released in 1978 and subsequently the recipient of numerous significant music-industry awards, "I Will Survive" has retained anthem status through the passing decades. It tells the story of a woman who, initially crushed by the desertion of her lover, comes to realize that she was just fine (better, in fact) without him, only to walk in and find him in her place, expecting her to take back his sorry ass. Oh, we don't *think* so.

J

Jack Rogers sandals, *noun*

Want to class up your dogs? Slip them into a pair of Jack Rogers sandals. More specifically, show them off in his iconic Navajo thongs—the stitched sandal that will forever be associated with the fiercely chic Jacqueline Kennedy Onassis. It's worth noting, however, that not all of us are in possession of Jackie O's dainty patrician peds, and these sandals are as narrow as a Klansman's mind. If your tootsies tend to spread out like a warm breakfast when released from their usual Chuck Taylors, the Navajo might not be the shoe for you.

Jawline Seam, *noun*

The bane of the foundation-wearing woman. Also known as the "shadow of doubt," the jawline seam is the visible line where the foundation color stops and your natural skin color begins. Depending on how liberally you apply your makeup, the jawline seam can range from a subtle shift in shade (from, for example, Barbados Bisque to Salt Lake City Sand) to a three-dimensional curb. In order to prevent being mistaken for someone who should be riding atop a parade float, first make sure your makeup color is a perfect match for your real skin tone and, second, take the time to blend, blend, blend your foundation—if necessary, all the way down to your hipbones.

Jeans, *noun*

"I'm going jeans shopping." It sounds so simple, doesn't it? You *fool.* Did you stock your purse with power bars and bottled water? Are you having a skinny day? Did you powder your thighs to prevent a friction seam-burn? Is your self-esteem at a seasonal high? Second only to swimsuit shopping, jeans shopping requires that you be at the top of your game, schooled in the silhouettes that flatter your body type, and impervious to even the cattiest salesclerk snark. Many's the woman who has casually strolled into the denim department without proper mental and physical preparation only to emerge two hours later, red-eyed, disoriented, and clutching a bag containing a pair of jeans that "seemed" to "work," only to discover at home that they have a lace-up fly and buttons for attaching rainbow suspenders.

Jeggings, *noun*

Created from the combination of jeans and leggings, jeggings are outrageously snug stretch-denim or faux-denim leggings that hovered on the fashion radar for approximately thirteen minutes in 2010. Some jeggings are made from materials that are similar to denim in texture; others are manufactured from the same fabric as tights but with a faux-jean graphic pattern applied after sewing. Jeggings possess the unique ability to distort even the sveltest figure into an appalling, irregular mass that polite society dictates must be covered by a long shirt or tunic.

Jewelry Party, *noun*

Also known in some areas as a Silpada party, this in-home sales event induces severe feelings of guilt and regret, either because you didn't buy enough merchandise to earn the hostess her freebie gift or because you were a little too transported by the Kenny G playing in the background and blew your entire car payment on *two* pairs of earrings. The considerate hostess anticipates these scenarios and provides a well-stocked spread of brie, crackers, and chardonnay, which allows you to avoid the shopping portion of the event or temporarily distracts the part of your brain that remembers how much you just spent.

JFL, *acronym*

Also adorably known as "jiffles" or "the jiffles," this is an acronym for the delightful state of dishevelment that results after a vigorous bout of lovemaking. Characteristics of the jiffles include mussed hair, smeared makeup, half-tucked shirt, swollen lips, flushed skin, and a happily dazed and bleary grin. Although there are other ways to interpret it, we like to think of these three letters as standing for the "Just Fluffed Look."

> **Fun***fact* The jiffles have been known to evoke both intense curiosity as well as envy among observers.

Jorts, *noun*

A combination of the words "jean" and "shorts," jorts are, shockingly, jean shorts. So far, so good. Beyond this basic definition, however, things get a little murky. Although some feel that jorts include any manner of denim short regardless of length, others describe jorts as strictly of the knee-length, baggy variety. Then there is the question of jort-genesis, or the manner in which the jorts were created. Were they initially manufactured as jorts or were they spontaneously formed by cutting off a pair of full-length jeans? And, just when you think you've got a handle on the whole jort situation, the question of age arises: are they jorts only if the wearer is above the age of, say, forty? Or are they jorts from birth 'til death and all the jort-sporting good times in between? And—wait—do we even like these things, whatever they are?

Judy Moody, *proper noun*

Borrowing its name from the popular children's books, a Judy Moody is a woman so volatile and so, well, moody, that you never know how she is going to treat you. Every encounter with Judy Moody is fresh and exciting—an emotional crap shoot that is as likely to leave you wondering why she's hugging you around the neck as wondering if this is the day she slipped a hunting knife into her purse and is planning to send you to that big shoe department in the sky. Yesterday everything was fine—why is she so angry at you today? Answer: there is no why. There is no yesterday. There is only you, Judy Moody, and whatever martial arts training you happen to have. Good luck.

Jumpsuit, *noun*

Unless you happen to be Evel Knievel, the jumpsuit is a treacherous item of clothing. Indeed, it is difficult to name another garment on which accurate tailoring is as critical. After all, what other outfit is capable of inflicting physical injury if the torso length is even half an inch too short? Now that we think about it, wearing that jumpsuit (which was made of leather—a notoriously nonstretch material) may have played a large part in giving Evel Knievel the courage to make those death-defying jumps on his motorcycle. Perhaps he was thinking, "Hell, I'm already wearing a leather jumpsuit. How much worse could my day get?"

Junk, *noun*

A slang term for genitalia that almost always refers to that of the male, specifically. When used in reference to a woman, however, it typically is a meditation on how much of said junk she happens to have in her "trunk" (*see also:* booty). Whereas some women express concern over what they feel is an excess amount of junk in their trunks, others feel they are lacking in this regard and seek to enhance the appearance of junk in their trunks, either through adjustments in dietary habits (*see also:* carbs) or through the use of a specialized, junk-enhancing undergarment (*see also:* butt bra).

Just Friends, *phrase*

Not to be confused with remaining friends, this is an entirely different concept. Exquisitely flexible in its meaning, the sentence "We're just friends" often means that the two people in question are, indeed, simply friends. Then again, those same three words can also mean that they are having sweaty lemur sex on parking level four every day at lunch and you are the last person in the department to catch on to that fact. Note: if two people are often asked whether they are "just friends," that's pretty solid evidence that they are more than "just friends."

Just Kidding, Love You, *phrase*
This is another phrase that pretends to mean the opposite of what it says (*see also:* I hate you), thus allowing the speaker to "take back" the lousy thing she just said to you. For example, "Chloe, you're such a bitch—just kidding, love you!" In order for the speaker to make this line work, the phrase must be accompanied by an aggressive smile and must immediately follow the insult or, better yet, be welded right onto it, as in, "Your hair looks so stupid todayjustkiddingloveyou!"

K

Kegel, *noun*

An internal exercise named for Dr. Arnold Kegel that involves repeated clenching of the pelvic muscles. Many women seek to increase the muscle strength in and around the pelvic floor for reasons such as recovery from childbirth, prevention of bladder leakage during sneezing and laughing, and heightened sensation during intercourse. Kegel exercises can be done with the use of a pelvic toning device (in the form of balls or other shapes inserted in the vagina for pushing resistance) or you can simply "freestyle" it by clenching your muscles anywhere, anytime. Many doctors recommend that women use stop-lights as reminders and make a practice of doing repetitive Kegels until the light turns green. It is unclear whether this practice has led to an increase or decrease in incidents of road rage in this country.

Knitting, *noun*

A popular fiber craft that has been around for centuries and continues to enjoy resurgences with each passing decade. A highly portable pastime, knitting requires only specialized needles and yarns of choice to create almost any item in just about any color/fiber combination.

Although knitting is a traditional craft with relatively homespun beginnings, the hobby has been taken up by a number of celebrities in recent years, leading to yet another surge in the craft's popularity. Although most women claim that knitting is a simple skill that can quickly be picked up even by the most uncoordinated novice, others find it to be virtually impossible to learn, even at the most rudimentary level. And we happen to know that they really, *really* tried. They even stayed after class at the yarn shop to ask for extra help while those other show-offs snickered at them. That's right—they heard the snickering.

Knockoff, *noun*
A knockoff is an illegal, counterfeit copy of a luxury item such as a designer watch or handbag. Often sold in sketchy parts of town or at "purse parties" hosted in private homes, knockoffs can be found in circulation across all income strata. Although we're the last ones to reproach a woman for faking it now and then (*see also:* boobs, lips, nails, hair, and faking it), there's nothing like the humiliation of having someone point out that your handbag appears to have been made by "Louie Vweeton" or "Prado."

Kryptonite Guy, *noun*
The one man in your life, past or present, against whom your womanly superpowers are useless. No matter how many tough talks your friends give you, no matter how many times you swear him off for good, you are a sitting duck for this guy, again and again. Although friends and family are unable to see or understand this man's otherworldly appeal, its effect on you is devastating, leaving your emotional compass spinning and your emotions roiling. The best you can hope for is that his hair falls out. But you know it won't. Dammit.

L

Labia, *noun*

Who makes this stuff up? Seriously, how did this brainstorming session go, exactly? Here you have this incredibly intimate, erotic part of a woman's body—the very gateway into the sexual and reproductive realm—and the best we've got is labia? Labia sounds like something growing in your armpit that needs to be lanced. And, please, don't trot out that old "it comes from Latin" line again. Haven't we blamed enough on the Romans? They're not even around to defend themselves. No, we need to step up, acknowledge that this name stinks, and come up with a better one. Like "threshold of awesomeness." Hey, it's just a jumping-off point.

Labor Day Rule, *noun*

The traditional fashion dictum that Labor Day heralds the beginning of fall and therefore the point after which it is no longer appropriate to wear such specifically "summer" items as white shoes, slacks, jackets, and handbags. The "no white after Labor Day" rule is still strictly observed in certain parts of the country while flagrantly ignored in others, particularly those that have little to no winter weather. In fact, in certain balmy, beachside communities, even the long-standing "no flip-flops on Christmas" rule has been abandoned.

Ladies' Room, *noun*

International port of refuge for females of all ages, the ladies' room is many things to many women. This single-sex sanctuary can serve as 1) a cooling-off zone after a spat, 2) a convenient space in which to freshen one's makeup or adjust an errant contact lens, 3) a compartment of solitude during a chatter-filled excursion, 4) a private location in which to discuss ongoing social developments with female companions, or 5) an escape hatch with an easy-to-open window for women on particularly horrific dates. Apparently, you can even tinkle in there. Although men often grouse about the amount of time it takes for a woman to return from a trip to the ladies' room, we understand that these complaints are merely an expression of envy at the intriguing aspect of our lifestyle that is *the ladies' room.*

Ladies Who Lunch, *noun*

Even before there were restaurants, there were the ladies who lunch. After all, who better to organize a silent-auction fundraiser to save the dinosaurs? As the millennia passed and the earth experienced radical climate fluctuations, these well-appointed ladies adapted by slipping on their cashmere cardigans or signaling for the waiter to tilt the blinds and diffuse the direct sunlight on the table. In recent history, the ladies who lunch have thrived as society has made critical advancements in valet-parking sciences and dressing-on-the-side technology.

Lady Butt, *noun*

Disorienting to men and women alike, lady butt occurs when a man's derriere is indistinguishable from a woman's when viewed from, um, behind. Coined during the 2010 Winter Olympics, the term received heavy use during the men's skiing competitions as the form-fitted ski suits required for the sport have a tendency to accentuate and amplify any existing feminine qualities in a man's bottom. For example: "I thought that was Lindsey Vonn until he turned around. Man, that dude has got some wicked lady butt."

Lady of Your Station, *phrase*

A phrase that is used to denote a woman's genteelness and to point out that perhaps she has or is about to stray into an activity or environment that is beneath her in some respect. This phrase is typically uttered by a concerned companion as a way of gently persuading the woman in question to reconsider her current course of action before suffering perhaps irreparable damage to her reputation. For example, a concerned companion might say, "Begging your pardon, Your Majesty, but it might be best if a lady of your station were not photographed by the press whilst holding her beer bong."

Ladywood, *noun*

A slang term for female sexual arousal in a general sense, presumably a play on the practice of calling a male erection a "woody." Taken a step further, ladywood can refer specifically to the physical swelling of the clitoris and surrounding labia during arousal. Then again, if you take two giant steps back, the term can be used much more generally about anything you find very appealing, as in, "Damn, those platform Louboutins are giving me ladywood—I must have them!"

Landing Strip, *noun*
The Indiana Jones of pubic topiary, the landing strip is an ideal choice for today's wash-n-go girl, offering clean, classic lines and a reasonable upkeep schedule. A utilitarian look that works on everyone from grad student to grandma, the landing strip consists of a neat stripe of hair about yay big that bisects the mons and is easily concealed by even the skimpiest bikini bottom. Travel enthusiasts take note: the landing strip has by far the most transportation-oriented name of all the pubic topiary designs.

Layers, *noun*
As with bangs (*see also:* bangs), the decision to cut layers into your hair is one not to be taken lightly as it has long-term consequences that are determined by a variety of factors. For example, do you have fuzzy, curly, or flyaway hair? If so, it's likely that layers, particularly dramatic ones, will completely ruin your life. (Yes, of course it looks great when you're leaving the salon—that's how they get you!) Seriously, you're going to need hats, and lots of them. On the other hand, do you have pin-straight hair that flows like a silk curtain whether you blow-dry it or not? Okay, that's super annoying.

LBD, *acronym*
Acronym for "little black dress," a universally acknowledged staple of a woman's wardrobe and one of the most versatile items of clothing you're likely to own. The intrinsic power of the LBD is that it looks

like a million bucks on you whether you're taking a post-brunch seaside stroll or working the red carpet at a premiere. Beyond versatility, however, is the LBD mystique—the one that telegraphs that you are the kind of fashion assassin who can reach into her closet on a moment's notice and effortlessly whip out not a bowling shirt, not a prairie skirt, but a little black number that looks to have been custom-made to showcase your figure. Note: this kind of woman also has a statistically high likelihood of owning a train case and/or having a knack for putting her hair up in a flawless French twist (*see also:* train case, French twist).

Leather Pants, *noun*

A clothing item that carries a degree-of-difficulty rating of ten (out of ten, btw), leather pants are both unforgiving (*see also:* old lady butt) and iconic (*see also:* Jim Morrison). The rule of thumb is that there *is* a perfect pair of these pants out there for you, but you will never find them. Studies have shown that, in order to optimize your chances of wearing leather pants without experiencing critical reputation fail, you must meet the following criteria: 1) you are twenty to twenty-five years old, *and* 2) you have a recording contract, *and* 3) you will be the subject of a critically acclaimed biopic later in life, *or* 4) you are Chrissie Hynde of The Pretenders.

Leg Warmers, *noun*

Like the beret, leg warmers are an item of clothing that beckons again and again . . . and again and again you must ask yourself, just as you do with regard to the beret: "Can I pull this off?" Let us help you: no, you cannot. This is a non-negotiable answer, with three exceptions: 1) you are a member of the American Ballet

Theatre or similarly revered repository of The Dance, 2) you are Jennifer Beals, 3) it is the eighties. (Note: items two and three above must occur *in tandem* in order to qualify for the exception to the leg warmers rule.)

-licious, *suffix*

A wonderfully versatile suffix that adds an extra layer of appeal (*see also:* BAM) to just about anything. Believed to have been spawned by the popularity of Beyoncé's hit song "Bootylicious," -licious began showing up at the ends of words that had never before been modified in this way, such as fabulicious, boobalicious, and discolicious. Like many pop cultural juggernauts, -licious could not be contained but rather gained momentum as it moved beyond its original use and into virgin pockets of the language, eventually migrating as far as baconlicious, sudokulicious, and polkalicious.

Lingerie, *noun*

From the French root word that can be roughly translated as "swank drawers," lingerie comprises women's underthings that mean business. Just as a men's silk pocket square is, as the expression goes, "for showin,' not for blowin'," lingerie is designed not with utilitarian intent, but rather to make a statement. Unlike the pocket square, however, the statement is not a public one, but rather intended for a more targeted audience, the headcount of which is a woman's private prerogative. What is lingerie's statement, exactly? For some, it is an expression of power, femininity, fantasy, or even fetish. For many, it is also an expression of really wanting to change into something more comfortable.

Lip Liner, *noun*

This is one of those cosmetic products whose appropriate use varies greatly with age, as in *your* age. Thanks to the blinding bloom of youth, teens and young women can get away with pretty much anything when it comes to makeup and hair. As a woman becomes more mature, however, certain practices become risky and, with the passage of yet more time, they become downright frightening. Thick, pancake makeup and shocking pink blush are two examples that come to mind, and lip liner is right there with them (*see also:* shaky lip liner). So please do your grandmother a favor and gently guide her away from the dark brown lip liner and toward a nice, elegant gloss. That way the younger children will stop asking where Nana's hiding the chocolate.

Lip Plumper, *noun*

A cosmetic product created with the intention of inflaming your lips so they swell and appear fuller. As plump, pouty lips continue to be a focus of the beauty and cosmetic industries, there is no shortage of lip-plumping glosses, gels, and sheens on the market. These products contain either natural or artificial ingredients that basically annoy, antagonize, taunt, or bitch-slap your lips. Your lips do their best to turn the other cheek, but eventually they react, swelling with anger. Depending on how strong the lip-plumping product is, your lips can stay pissed off for hours.

Lipstick Trick, *noun*

A handy maneuver that can be performed anywhere, anytime in order to help prevent lipstick from being accidentally deposited on one's teeth (*see also:* Cujo syndrome). To do the lipstick trick, apply your lipstick as usual. Then, make an "O" with your lips and insert your (clean) pointer finger into the center of the "O" without touching your lips. Gently close your lips around your finger and pull your finger outward, away from your face. Using a tissue, wipe any excess lipstick from your finger. On second thought, this may be a maneuver that is best performed in the privacy of one's home or car.

Liquid Eyeliner, *noun*

When it comes to makeup application, liquid eyeliner is the great equalizer. Sure, you're handy with the mascara wand. You know your way around an eyebrow pencil. But have you got *skillz? What's the big deal?* you ask. *It's just like any other eyeliner.* Don't be a chump. You think watching a couple of instructional videos on You-Tube is going to get you through this? Do you understand that the slightest miscalculation—the merest whiff of a wobble—turns you in a heartbeat from Audrey Hepburn to Marilyn Manson? And forget starting over or trying to fix it if you go astray. You might as well be drawing rings around your eyes with a Sharpie.

Lobster Heels, *noun*

The condition that exists when a woman allows her heels to become so hard and scaly that they resemble a lobster's crusty exterior. Mild-to-moderate cases of lobster heels can be remedied relatively easily with brisk exfoliation (*see also:* exfoliation) and the application of an intense moisturizer. Advanced lobster heels, however, can become so rough and cracked that they require repeated treatments with a motorized sanding device and specialized lubricants formulated to ease your heels out of their crustacean condition and return them to their original mammalian state. During this period of transition, it is recommended that you shroud your feet in rain boots or tube socks when in public because, seriously, no one wants to see those things.

M

Maiden Name, *noun*

Traditionally, a woman's family or birth name that she uses until she has occasion to change it as a result of, for example, marriage. Although many modern maidens choose to retain their birth names in some form regardless of marital status, others cleave to tradition and take their husbands' names, often permanently abandoning their original surnames.

> **Fun***fact* A woman's maiden name can make a reappearance through the use of the word "née," meaning "born as" (example: Geraldine Lang née Fong). However, it is estimated that 86 percent of people have no idea what this means.

Maid of Honor, *noun*

A crucial yet underappreciated job, the maid of honor serves as the bride's right-hand woman both during the wedding and in the months leading up to it. The maid of honor should expect to be called upon at any time to step into the role of crisis counselor, seamstress, EMT, beautician, chauffeur, or Navy Seal. In return, she will receive a crappy faux-sterling box onto which her initials have been engraved off-center and which will begin to cloud around the corners within three months. Note: in keeping with tradition, the bride will tell the rest of the bridal party that it was the maid of honor who insisted on the dresses with the heinous butt bow (*see also:* butt bow).

Makeover, *noun*

A high-stakes experiment in which you turn your appearance over to someone whose last job, for all you know, was as a stylist on the kiddie-pageant circuit. Done skillfully, the makeover can result in a polished, more confident you while passing on new skills to bring out the best in your appearance every day. The other 97 percent of the time, however, the makeover leaves you gaping in stunned silence at the grotesquely glazed she-clown in the mirror and wondering how you're going to get your $400 worth of new makeup home without being accused of working another girl's corner.

Makeunder, *noun*

A process by which a woman's "look" is toned down and simplified by a professional, resulting in a redesigned appearance that is softer, more natural, and closer to her original default setting. The *typical* candidate for a makeunder is a woman who applies her makeup with too liberal a hand, styles her hair in a distracting or unattractive manner, or wears clothes that could be described as unflattering or over the top. The *ideal* candidate for a makeunder does all three of these simultaneously, most likely while upending a bottle of perfume into her cleavage.

Mall Crawl, *noun*
A routine trip to the mall for the purpose of, um, going to the mall. Typically undertaken in the company of at least one girlfriend, the mall crawl is to modern times what a stroll down the avenue was at the turn of the century—a chance to see and be seen, to pass the time while exchanging bits of news and gossip, to trade evasive barbs with the pushy guy who runs the hand-massage kiosk, and to eat frozen yogurt. "What are you here to get, exactly?" a male might ask, thereby disclosing that he does not understand what malls are for *at all*. Like Mt. Everest, the mall is crawled because it is *there*.

Mammogram, *noun*
A delightful, relaxing procedure in which a woman's breast is pressed between two plates until it is approximately a micron thick and the size of a patio table, then bombarded with X-rays, yielding an inscrutable image that resembles the opposite of a breast. Bonus features of the mammogram experience may include a drafty waiting room, nonvalidated parking, gruff staff, and unlimited easy listening music. It is recommended that women over the age of thirty-five receive a mammogram annually, but many women "cheat" and schedule several examinations per year just because it is so much dang fun.

Mandatory Waiting Period, *noun*
The magical, non-negotiable length of time that a man feels he must wait to contact a woman following a first date. The exact period of

time may vary from man to man, but on average ranges anywhere from twenty-four hours to a week. From a woman's point of view, this kind of rigid, arbitrary practice is a total steaming pantload, with flaws both obvious and numerous. For example, if you had a great date, why torment yourself while other men with thicker, more lustrous hair move in on the future mother of your children? On the other hand, if she's the kind of woman who's Google-street-viewing your house and looking for an easy entry point as we speak, why risk pissing her off?

Man Drought, *noun*
An extreme scarcity of eligible men. Woe to the single woman who, for whatever reason, finds herself in the midst of a man drought. For some, it occurs because they have chosen a career that does not happen to draw as many men as women, effectively cutting themselves off from a primary pipeline of potential mates. Other women may make the misstep of settling into a bedroom community populated primarily by young families, whereas others awaken to the unhappy discovery that they have accidentally enrolled in a women's college. Regardless of her individual circumstances, today's single woman hones her social meteorology skills, ready to migrate to more fertile climes at the first sign of a dreaded man drought.

Man Hands, *noun*
Launched into the popular vernacular by the legendary sitcom *Seinfeld*, the term man hands describes a woman's hands that, for one reason or another, look like they should be at the end of a man's arms rather than a woman's. Characteristics that trigger the man hands label include finger beefiness, excessive and/or ropey veininess,

general coarseness, and, of course, overall size. Although there is no cure for the condition of man hands, an effective optical illusion that helps make the hands appear smaller can be created by wearing giant rings, bracelets, and watches. And, unless you're going trick-or-treating as Minnie Mouse, leave the white gloves in the drawer.

Manicure, *noun*

A nail service conducted by a professional that typically includes the following steps: 1) you wait in the corner along with several tense, glaring women for your nail professional to become available while you thumb through the August 1988 issue of *Vogue*, 2) you begin your manicure with polish removal, finger soaking, and small talk, gently correcting the manicurist whose questions make it apparent that she has confused you with another client who was a dancer in *Cats* and is married to an accordionist, 3) you try in vain to find a neutral place to look while receiving your hand/forearm massage, 4) you watch the application of the polish, which always turns out to be too dark, too light, too sheer, too goth, or too trashy, 5) you wreck three to five of your freshly painted nails trying to get your keys out of your purse.

Mani-Pedi, *noun*

A shorthand term for a combination manicure-pedicure, the use of which marks the speaker as an experienced nail salon vet. The mani-pedi client visit to the salon has all the earmarks of a maintenance pit stop during the Daytona 500—you know the crew, you know the drill, and you need to get your wheels back out on the pavement as soon as possible so let's hustle. Brisk and efficient, the mani-pedi is certain to pave the way for other convenient procedure combinations in the future, such as the hearing testie–ear piercey and the gynie-waxie.

Man Purse, *noun*
Not to be confused with a briefcase, messenger bag, or satchel, the man purse is a smallish, handbag-like accessory made specifically for men to contain and tote their "stuff," and which may include a shoulder strap or, conversely, be designed to be carried in the hand as a clutch. Some women can overlook this gender-bending fashion practice in the short-term, choosing instead to concentrate on the manlier qualities of their companions while silently praying that the purse thing extinguishes itself before they run into anyone they know. Most women, however, will balk at the first flash of the man purse, which triggers a rapid recalibration and subsequent downgrading of relationship potential. The appearance of the man purse also introduces the substantive and troubling question: "What is it, exactly, that this man carries around that requires a case while other men do just fine with their pants pockets?"

Manscaping, *noun*
A men's grooming practice through which facial and/or body hair is tamed, maintained, beaten back, and shaped with the goal of creating a more polished appearance. Manscaping can include, but is not limited to, shaving, trimming, clipping, tweezing, and waxing. Women's attitudes regarding manscaping are as varied as the array of hair patterns a man can produce on his chin, but it is generally true that each woman has a personal "point of no return" past which manscaping is no longer alluring but feels like a personal challenge, as in, "What the hell? His eyebrows look neater than mine!"

Marionette Lines, *noun*
You're nobody's puppet and, as far as we're concerned, the less you
resemble one, the better. That's why those creases that run from
the corners of your mouth to the sides of your nose have got to go.
Jiminy Cricket! It's time to escape the Island of Lost Girls and make
an appointment at Dr. Geppetto's workshop where, if you wish upon
a star, he'll fill those lines right where they are. After all, you're made
of awesome, not maple.

Martha Stewart, *proper noun*
Exacting overlord of all things pertaining to homemaking/cooking/
crafting whose name you invoke when you want to act like you're
giving someone a compliment but really you're letting her know that
you're sick and tired of her making everyone else— including you—
look like crap. Example: "Well, aren't you Martha Stewart, making
your own felted-flower bow to go on that birthday gift!" Translation:
"Only a flagrant passive-aggressive would spend four hours making
an organic felt bow and, let me guess, you also handmade the wrapping paper using only a screen door and a potato, right? Go to hell!"

Masturbation, *noun*
The act of sexually pleasuring oneself, typically through the manipu-
lation of the genitals and to the point of orgasm (*see also:* orgasm).
Whether you consider masturbation a hobby, occasional pastime,
hardcore sport, or something you find yourself doing more often
than you check your e-mails, this highly satisfying practice has
something for everyone. Offering a complimentary and spontaneous mini-vacation/in-flight-movie/spa treatment/tension releaser, all
provided by the one person who knows your preferences better than

anyone, masturbation is truly the gift you never have to give anyone but yourself. When you put it that way, who are we to tell you to knock it off?

Maven, *noun*

A word of Yiddish origin that has become increasingly—and exasperatingly—prevalent with the advent of social media. It is almost impossible to spend time on Twitter or Facebook without encountering the aggressive claims of various mavens such as marketing mavens, coupon mavens, etc. It is worth noting that all the cool maven jobs appear to be taken, with current openings available only for halitosis maven, frozen chicken nugget maven, and traffic school maven.

Maxi Dress, *noun*

Not to be confused with maxi pad (*see also:* maxi pad), the maxi dress is a floor-length (or longer) dress that is typically casual and may or may not be made of an eye-catching patterned fabric. Available in a boggling array of designs, the popular maxi dress offers the unique and useful features of hiding a wide variety of figure flaws, effectively obscuring most spray-tan mishaps, and providing a convenient as well as roomy cover for any leftover party food or centerpieces that you'd like to take home with you.

Maxi Pad, *noun*

Aircraft carrier of the menstrual fleet, the maxi pad comes in three sizes: huge, ginormous, and continental. Held in place decades ago (when it was known horrifyingly as a sanitary napkin) by an ungainly belt, today's maxi pads are designed with the modern woman in mind and are affixed to your lacy underthings by Space Age adhesive. Some pads even come wrapped in sassy colors to match your sassy uterus. Although there are many models of maxi pads on the market whose features address rates of flow, times of day, and winged-versus-flightless classification, the primary function of this level of feminine protection is to absorb Lake Superior while its wearer continues blithely to do the Dougie.

Menopause, *noun*
Term for the phase of life in which a woman's ovaries officially retire, at which point they are taken out to lunch, given a gold watch in gratitude for their years of faithful service, and sent home to change into elastic-waist pants and start boning up on things like herb gardening and writing angry letters to the editor of the local weekly. This can be a tricky transition for many women, especially those who are not accustomed to bursting into flames without warning (*see also:* hot flash). For many, however, menopause signals a welcome transition into a stage of life that leaves behind the nuisance of menstruation (*see also:* Festival of Menses, Aunt Flo) and ushers in an era of increased confidence and contentment— a state that is much more likely to endure if you never *ever* look up "menopause" on the Internet.

Merkin, *noun*
A small "wig" or patch of hair, feathers, or sequins affixed to the pubic area. The merkin has been around for hundreds of years and got its start in showbiz while working in brothels, where it disguised the fact that the prostitutes had either shaved off their pubic hair for hygienic reasons or had lost it as a side effect of treatment for STDs.

More recently, the merkin has taken a higher-profile role on stage and screen where it is worn by performers either as a strategic cover-up or to conform to the historical pubic styles of the play or film's era, which may predate such contemporary pubic topiary arrangements as the landing strip and Hitler 'stache. Beyond the entertainment industry, the merkin can also be seen glistening in the sun at events with the most relaxed of dress codes, such as outdoor music festivals.

Messy Bun, *noun*
A cute, convenient, and easy up-do that works on any hair texture and can be created by even the most hair-inept. To make your own messy bun, simply gather your hair into a loose ponytail, twirl it into a bun, then wrap the hair tie of your choice around the bun to secure it. The messy bun can also be held in place by a strategically placed chip clip (*see also:* chip clip). Don't want to start with the ponytail? No problem! Just crush your hair into a wad and lock it in place with a tie or clip. Droopy bun? Great! Off-center bun? Very avant-garde! The beauty of the messy bun is that it's supposed to look casual, freeform, and, well, messy. Note: the "messy" aspect of the messy bun does not include add-ons such as grass clippings and bits of dried breakfast cereal (*see also:* nasty bun).

Metrosexual, *noun*
Although its exact origin is disputed, the term metrosexual is understood to refer to a man who embraces behaviors not usually attributed to the typical, "old-fashioned" male, such as paying acute attention to personal grooming and attire as well to more general issues of style, trends, and popular culture. An accomplished

shopper, the metrosexual stays on top of developments in the world of fashion and has exacting standards when it comes to purchases relating both to his appearance and his home. Although use of the term itself appears to be waning since its peak in 2005, metrosexuals continue to be a thriving, vibrant slice of society and can be observed in virtually every urban center, particularly in the shopping district.

MILF, *acronym*

An acronym for a crude phrase that roughly translates as "mom I'd like to 'friend in the extreme'," the MILF is as much a part of the contemporary social landscape as the corner gas station or coffee dispensary. Today's moms pride themselves on being fit, groomed, and engaged in the world outside the home. These developments have opened new sexual vistas for men who would never have given a second glance to the stereotypical moms of yesteryear. Whether she is aware of it or not, the MILF gathers appreciative looks from nearby men as she bends fetchingly over the side of the stroller to wipe the crusty nose of her sixteen-month-old, particularly from the men who either have unresolved issues with their mothers or who are frightened by unattached, available women.

Mohawk/Fauxhawk, *noun*

Two variations on a pubic topiary design theme in which the center ridge of pubic hair is shaped to stand straight up in an elevated stripe. In the Mohawk version, the hair on both sides of the stripe is waxed or shaved away, whereas the fauxhawk "fakes it" by leaving all the hair intact, but coaxing it to stand up in a ridge along its center. Based on an ancient hairstyle used by many cultures to intimidate their enemies when facing them in battle, it is not clear if the pubic Mohawk/fauxhawk is also worn to inspire fear in those who approach it.

Mom Jeans, *noun*
Catchall, derogatory term for unstylish, unflattering jeans that appear to place a higher value on utilitarian comfort than on fashion. Typically high-waisted (*see also:* high-waisted jeans) and/or baggy (but not in a good way), so-called mom jeans exist in a category all their own and are not linked to any particular style moment when they were sold in stores. Instead they seem to have appeared spontaneously in the back of a closet where they emerged, like the walking catfish, as a hiccup in denim's evolutionary chain.

Fun*fact* No one knows exactly how our nation's mothers got smeared with responsibility for this fashion offense, but as soon as the guilty parties are identified, you can bet they are going to be on one hell of a timeout.

Monogram, *noun*
In the context of a wedding, a monogram is often an artful depiction of the couple's initials used to decorate invitations, napkins, note cards, and other matrimonial gear. Outside of the wedding context, however, the monogram winks at you from the pages of a clothing catalog, raising questions in your mind and luring you toward the monogram lifestyle, the very idea of which gives you an uncontrollable urge to pop your collar, slip on deck shoes, and dump everything you own into a huge canvas tote. Resist the temptation.

Unfortunately, you neither own a sailboat nor enjoy lobster wrestling. Also, you live in New Mexico.

Mons, *noun*

1. Also known as the mons pubis, this is the cushion of tissue that lies atop a woman's pubic bone. Even cooler, it's also called the mons veneris or "mound of Venus." As the most readily visible portion of a woman's genital area, the mons serves as the canvas for any manner of artful sculpting of the pubic hair (*see also:* topiary). The mons serves as handy, built-in protection for the pubic bone during intercourse in the same way a stadium cushion protects your tailbone during playoff games, only sexier. **2.** A city in Belgium. (Random!)

Moobs, *noun*

A syllable-saving combination of "man" and "boobs," moobs is one of those words that, once you acquire it, you use it so much that it pays for itself in about three days. Why is this the case? Because moobs are everywhere—lolling at the beach, swinging at the gym, and winking playfully from the armholes of tank tops in the park. Not to be confused with pecs, moobs are the pliable, muscle-free mounds that hang in a decidedly breasty way on some men's chests regardless of age. Most women will agree that, even though there may well be a pair of them at home whose owner they adore, moobs are, as a rule, best kept under wraps in public.

Mrs. Potato Head, *noun*

1. A slang term for a woman who has had so many plastic surgery and/or facial rejuvenation procedures that she appears extremely artificial, as if she is comprised of separate, unrelated parts that have been haphazardly assembled. Mrs. Potato Head is typically blissfully unaware of others' reactions to the results of her aggressive beautification measures and takes their polite silence as tacit approval or even encouragement to undertake additional procedures. You know, Mrs. Potato Head, we thought you looked really pretty the way you were. **2.** Mr. Potato Head's wife.

Muffin Tops, *noun*
Irresistibly attractive yet widely misunderstood "dunes of delight" that can be found nestled above the waistbands of virtually every woman of healthy weight in the continental United States. (At least, the ones you would want to be friends with.) The presence of muffin tops has been positively correlated with such attributes as superior intellect, exquisite fashion sensibility, and shiny, manageable hair. Named for the portion of a muffin that bulges over the top of the muffin pan during baking, it is said that some muffin tops actually do emit the aroma of freshly baked bread.

Mustache, *noun*
The unwanted (*right!?*) hair on a woman's upper lip that can vary widely in color and density from a downy white-blonde fuzz to a brambly brunette thicket. For women who seek to remove or otherwise obscure their mustaches, a number of methods are available including bleaches, waxes, hair-dissolving creams, and handheld devices designed to rip the offending hairs out by their roots. It is worth noting that one's propensity for growing a mustache can change dramatically with age, leaving one with the disturbing notion that it's possible to go to bed as Kristen Stewart and wake up as Groucho Marx.

Mystery Friend, *noun*

The mystery friend is someone who greets you with over-the-top excitement and familiarity but whom you only vaguely remember. As she clamps a huge hug on you in the supermarket aisle, you wrack your brain trying to place her in your personal history. She looks like that girl from the scuba class you took before your Belize trip two years ago, but you hardly knew her. She sure knows *you*, though. She asks about your uncle's gall bladder surgery, your promotion at work, and whether you still suspect your yoga teacher is flirting with your boyfriend. Now she's suggesting that you two get together but *you're* wondering how long it's going to take her to realize you don't know her name.

N

Nails, *noun*

Short for "fingernails," this seems like a pretty simple concept . . . on the surface. There's nothing simple about a woman's nails, however, because even though they appear to be the same little tabs of keratin that are found on the ends of most humans' fingers, they are, in fact, ten tiny billboards that constantly send messages about their owner. Are you fancy, tough, high-maintenance? Do you follow trends or stay with understated classics? Are you into hardware such as tips, acrylics, and dangling charms? Would you never be caught outside your home with chipped polish or do you go for weeks between manicures? Bottom line: when it comes to gaining information about a woman, if you "talk to the hand," the hand will talk to you.

New Year's Eve, *noun*

One of two popular holidays (*see also:* Valentine's Day) saddled with huge societal expectations that, let's be honest here, never pan out. Unlike Valentine's Day, New Year's Eve seeks to move beyond the confines of your romantic life and make you feel like crap about pretty much *every* aspect of your existence. After all, what have you done with the past twelve months of your time? Gotten a promotion, lost that stubborn ten pounds, turned your idea for the GluteMistress 9000 into a personal fortune? And you think scrawling a list of resolutions on the back of a Der Wienerschnitzel bag is going to change something for you? Here, put this sequined thing on your head and drink this.

New Year's Resolutions, *noun*
The traditional set of personal commitments (usually oriented toward self-improvement) that many people make when looking ahead to the coming year (*see also:* gym membership). As the old saying goes, "Promises are made to be broken." Nowhere is this truer than in the case of New Year's resolutions which, scribbled earnestly on legal pads and cocktail napkins as midnight approaches, are largely abandoned in the cold light of January. After all, they're just promises you made to *yourself*, right? Who knows better than you just how hard you're trying? Walk to the mailbox instead of driving? Have dinner with your parents twice a year? Stop sending nude photos of yourself to your boyfriend's boss? Geez, who can live up to these kinds of expectations?

Nip Slip, *noun*
Short for "nipple slip," the nip slip occurs when one of your nipples escapes the article of clothing meant to contain it and makes for daylight, thus exposing itself to public view and likely exposing you, the owner, to extreme embarrassment. An occurrence that has been thoroughly documented thanks to the rise in the legions of paparazzi that observe all celebrities at all times, the nip slip raises several questions, such as *Who knew these little buggers were such a*

flight risk? and *Did this ever happen to Cleopatra?* Today, many busy women rely on the popular "Where Are Your Nipples?" iPhone app to track and monitor their breasts and help prevent unintentional public nipple viewings.

Not-So-Fresh Feeling, *noun*
Injected into the popular consciousness decades ago by an infamous series of douche commercials, the not-to-fresh feeling has been stalking females ever since. And, like many catch phrases that percolate through pop culture, its original source has become obscured and its meaning broadened, leaving many contemporary women wondering about the source and strength of this not-so-freshness. What if it has migrated from our lady parts to foul our armpits? Our breath? How can we be expected to concentrate on having sparkling smiles and volumized hair with this nonfresh funk hanging over us? And, keeping in mind the value that society places on female freshness in all forms (*see also:* freshness), what in God's name is to be done about it?

O

Office Spouse, *noun*

A person of the opposite sex to whom you are intimately connected in the workplace, but with whom you are not romantically involved. Your office spouse knows your habits, your food allergies, how you take your coffee, how to inspire you to excel, and how to build you back up after you've been crushed. Depending on your job, he or she may also be a better traveling companion than your real spouse. In fact, many people's relationships with their work spouses are happier, smoother, and more productive than any other relationships in their lives. That being said, it might be tempting to upgrade and expand your office spouse relationship to that of "real" spouse. Then again, why wreck it?

Old Lady Butt, *noun*

Not to be confused with lady butt (a men's condition), old lady butt occurs most often when your derriere is compressed within the confines of a tight or poorly cut garment, causing the entire region to appear withered or misshapen or, in extreme cases, to disappear altogether. Most notable to the condition is the apparent fusing of the two hemispheres of the butt into a single, unnatural-looking unit. Contrary to its name, old lady butt can strike a woman of any age and, for reasons that are not fully understood, the condition becomes critical if any attempt is made to wear leather pants.

One Night Stand, *noun*
A spontaneous sexual encounter that is acknowledged by both parties or—just as often—only one party, as being a one-off occurrence. Although the one night stand can provide emotional excitement, the thrill of pursuit, and sexual satisfaction, the distraction that accompanies these activities often results in an unfortunate lack of communication resulting in misunderstandings as to the status of the coupling and its classification on a going-forward basis. More often than not, it is the female participant who walks away from the one night stand (*see also:* walk of shame) under the mistaken impression that, rather than an exhilarating but terminal evening of sexual adventure, she has instead just launched a long-term and exclusive relationship (*see also:* bunny boiler).

One-Piece, *noun*
A shorthand term for a women's one-piece swimsuit, although no one ever says "one-piece swimsuit." To the female ear, a tidal wave of subtext is unleashed when a woman says that she's planning to wear a one-piece on an outing to, say, a beach or resort. Subtextual packets of information communicated by this statement include but are not limited to the following: 1) she is not currently feeling confident about her figure, 2) she is still skittish after the last outing when that big wave knocked her bottoms right off, 3) she has not completed her tramp stamp-removal treatments (*see also:* tramp stamp), 4) she

will be supervising small children on this outing, and 5) she will be swimming the English Channel.

Orgasm, *noun*

A term for sexual climax that can be applied to either gender. The highly prized orgasm can come about as a result of self-stimulation of the desired genital area(s) or stimulation of such areas by one or more other parties. Physiologically speaking, the orgasm includes deeply pleasurable muscle contractions along with increased blood pressure as well as heart and respiration rates. Neighborly speaking, the orgasm can also exhibit rhythmic wall and headboard thumping, boisterous repetitive chanting, shrieking of anything from profanities to the combination to your old bike lock, and prolonged nonverbal issuances ranging from moaning to staccato yelping to any of a variety of calls typically heard in nature's wilds.

Orgy, *noun*

A totally fantastical, made-up notion in which a bunch of people—strangers, even!—meet up, take off their clothes, and have all different kinds of sex and snack foods. Although this is a wildly appealing concept, we all know that no one has these supposed get-togethers because if they did, statistically speaking, we would have been invited to one by now. And so, while it's fun to fantasize for a short time about spectacular things we wish were true, it's probably best to move on and stop thinking about this thing called an orgy, which, as we've established, does not exist.

Overconfirmer, *noun*

A male who needs constant reassurance that his female companion is, in fact, having a good time. The overconfirmer's arsenal of inquiries is a hefty one, allowing him to launch frequent queries throughout an evening, including, "Are you having fun?" "Is this all right?" "Aren't you glad we did this?" and "This is great, huh?" Some women may enjoy dating a man who takes on the persona of an overly solicitous maitre d', however, it is generally acknowledged that most women will, after a prolonged barrage of these inquiries, respond in a manner that is startlingly similar to that of a wild boar repeatedly prodded with a sharp stick.

Overeager, *adjective*

This term is the flipside of playing hard-to-get (*see also:* hard-to-get) and describes a woman who makes herself too available to a man she finds attractive, thus violating the widely accepted cardinal rule of dating, which states that the male shall be the chaser and the female shall be the chased. The term overeager is most often found in the vicinity of phrases such as "stop throwing yourself at him" and "make him work for it," all of which are likely to be spoken to the woman in question by another, caring female. (*Hi, Mom.*) Examples of overeager behavior could include posting nude photos of yourself on his Facebook page, cruising past his house every fifteen minutes while blasting that Taylor Swift song, and inquiring whether he has strong feelings about hot air-balloon weddings.

Over-the-Knee Boots, *noun*

No longer just for sword-fighting cats, over-the-knee boots can be seen on everyone from fourth graders to soccer moms to seniors kickin' it in Denny's at 6:00 A.M. on a Tuesday. We're not saying we're happy about it, but those are the facts. Much like leather pants (*see also:* leather pants), over-the-knee boots are ideally suited for a very slender segment of the general population. A segment so slender, in fact, that if it turned sideways you wouldn't be able to see it at all.

P

Pageant Hair, *noun*

A notoriously rigid, voluminous hairdo that looks like an excessively "fixed" arrangement rather than a casual, everyday style. Named for the furiously teased and sprayed hair helmets that were seen on the beauty contest circuit in decades past and can still occasionally be seen today, pageant hair attracts attention from its combination of theatricality and retro fierceness. It's worth noting that, whereas intentional pageant hair takes both applied effort and applied hair spray, you can inadvertently create a style that is pageant-adjacent simply by overteasing, cross-combing, and/or spritzing on one too many clouds of hair spray. In the event of accidental pageant hair, stylists advise that you embrace your creation, select your wardrobe accordingly, and *work it.*

Panticlimber, *noun*

Also known as a "parade float," this is a term for a pantiliner that, for one reason or another, has come unstuck from its assigned spot in the crotch of the panties and has meandered upward into a new, nonapproved location. The release of a panticlimber is often the result of strenuous athletic activity such as basketball or volleyball. The adhesion of the beached pantiliner to the skin in its new location can cause considerable discomfort, the symptoms of which can include a marked decrease in athletic performance, repeated attempts at clothing adjustment, and a noticeably altered gait.

Pantiliner, *noun*

If the maxi pad is an aircraft carrier, the pantiliner (also known as a panty liner or the more warlike panty shield) is a canoe. Slender and lightweight, the pantiliner clings to the gusset (WTF?) of your undies like a fond memory—barely there but reassuring nonetheless.

> **Fun***fact* Many forms of feminine protection are available in nondisposable cloth that can be laundered and reused (*see also:* this is where more than one woman's environmentalism gets thrown right out of the van). Also, for the sake of accuracy, we are required to include the words "scented," "discharge," and "incontinence" in this definition, but we're not happy about it.

Panty Lines, *noun*

Also known as "visible panty lines," these are the traces of your underwear elastic that can be seen through the fabric of your pants or skirt, alerting observers as to the exact style and location of said drawers. As if that weren't mortifying enough, panty lines also perform a second disservice by pressing into all but the hardest of bun cheeks and, by dividing them into freeform segments, highlighting any squishiness thereof. Panty lines can be eradicated by the application of a thong (*see also:* thong) or, if a scorched-earth approach is preferred, going commando (*see also:* commando).

Parentheses, *noun*
Named for their resemblance to the punctuation pair often seen in English sentences (like this), "parentheses" is plastic surgery slang for the set of curved lines that often appears near the sides of a woman's mouth. Impossible to camouflage with makeup (*see also:* spackle), parentheses are most effectively counteracted with injectable "fillers." It's worth noting that you do not have to speak parenthetically in order to earn a pair of these creases, nor do you have to exhibit even a rudimentary understanding of punctuation marks and their uses.

Pashmina, *noun*
People just love to say "pashmina." Why? Because it makes them sound fancy. Whether or not you agree, you have to admit that the term is preferable to the generic "wrap" and certainly to the geriatric "shawl." This rectangular accessory, which is available in an almost infinite combination of sizes, colors, and patterns, can add a touch of feminine elegance to even the most tragic of outfits. Technically, a pashmina is supposed to be cashmere, but once you cut the tags off, who's to know?

Pearls, *noun*
Pearls, particularly in necklace form, comprise one of the most iconic categories of jewelry ever conceived. So iconic, in fact, that they deliver a single unwavering message: respectability. Oh, sure, you can plaster diamonds onto a skull and people will say "edgy,"

but you slide a few pearls onto a necklace made of human teeth and suddenly someone's wearing it with a St. John knit suit to a Junior League meeting and no one bats an eye.

Pedicure, *noun*
If done correctly, the pedicure is like sex for your feet: a stimulating yet relaxing interlude during which someone is completely focused on delivering pleasure to your body or a targeted portion thereof. If done incorrectly, the pedicure is like sending your feet to a women's prison where you are expected to tip the warden. Keeping this in mind, it is crucial to select a quality pedicure provider, as for every toasty sea salt and lotus-blossom soak tub there is an equal and opposite dingy plastic pan filled with a tepid broth of dishwashing soap.

Pencil Skirt, *noun*
Named for its straight, slender silhouette, the pencil skirt is a very popular garment with women who appreciate classic, body-skimming style. It's worth noting, however, that unless you're buying the skirt for your twelve-year-old son, you can expect to make a trip to the tailor because, as a rule, women are not shaped like pencils.

Fun*fact* The pencil skirt was known as the "H-line" skirt for about five minutes back in the forties. Unofficial garment of hot librarians everywhere, the pencil skirt almost demands that you wear your hair in a stern bun until the opportunity presents itself to shake it loose to the accompaniment of some *shicka-BOW* music.

Pencil Test, *noun*

A simple, at-home method for assessing the buoyancy and/or altitude of your breasts. Remove clothing, then gently lift one (1) of your breasts. With your free hand, hold a pencil against your chest at the base of your breast, parallel with your waistband. Release your breast and then release the pencil as well. The pencil will either be held in place by the fold of the breast or it will clatter to the floor. What do these results mean? We have no idea. We're not even sure why we're doing this test in the first place. We were just curious.

Perfume, *noun*

An aromatic concoction worn by many women which, when applied with restraint, creates a pleasing fragrance experience for those in close proximity. Applied too liberally, however, perfume becomes a nasal assault weapon, with collateral damage to the eyes and even taste buds of those within striking distance. The exact footprint of a perfuming varies with atmospheric pressure, prevailing winds, and, of course, the brand of the fragrance in question. Lighter, fruity scents tend to dissipate within a reasonable amount of time, whereas heavy florals and musks have been known to render elevator lobbies unusable for an entire afternoon.

Perfume Spritzer, *noun*

We've all seen them in the cosmetics department, those women strategically stationed next to makeup counters and lurking behind garish displays, ready to leap from cover like overly accessorized ninjas and nail passersby with an unwelcome stream of Musky Orchid Grenade or whatever scent they happen to be hawking. Sociologists have long marveled at the persistence of this practice, which is openly reviled by consumers and which turns a pleasant afternoon of shopping into an evolutionary exercise as the spritzers take down the slower, weaker members of the retail herd while only the crafty and fleet-of-foot make it to the escalator and the safety of the housewares department beyond.

Period, *noun*

A woman's monthly menstrual cycle (*see also:* Aunt Flo, Festival of Menses). Damn, it's great to be a woman. And, so you don't forget just how great it is, your body reminds you each month by trying to eject a portion of your insides onto your new white pants. The downside of this arrangement is obvious. The upside, however, is that if you can go about your business—earning a living, holding up your end of your relationships, laughing, helping others, etc.—while spending a quarter of that time bleeding voluminously and never letting on, well, lady, you can do *anything*.

Perm, *noun*

An abbreviation of "permanent wave," the term refers to an ancient hair treatment process that is still in use in remote areas of the United States. The application of the perm involves winding the hair tightly onto small spools then soaking the hair and scalp in a broth of chemicals that smells like the missing Easter egg your dog found two months later behind the gardening shed. Once released from the curlers, the hair takes on the texture of electrified mattress stuffing and retains this quality until it is eventually sheared off following a rocky "growing-out period." Perms can be classified in two categories: the "salon perm" and a particularly virulent strain known as the "home perm."

Pilates, *noun*

Developed in Germany in the early twentieth century, Pilates is a system of physical training that emphasizes smooth, controlled movements and development of core strength through the use of equipment that looks like it belongs in the back room of a large-animal veterinarian. Designer Joseph Pilates dubbed his fitness method Contrology and stressed the importance of the mind-body connection, particularly in the form of intense mental concentration during each exercise. Hey, someone should make an app for that! Wait, what were we talking about?

Pinky, *noun*

Of all your fingers, the pinkies are by far the snootiest, each holding approximately 48 percent of your body's superiority (the remaining 4 percent residing in the tip of your nose). Studies have shown that merely by raising either pinky to half-staff, your social judgment threat level (as perceived by neutral observers) doubles. A pinky that is hoisted to the full vertical position as an accompaniment to other gestures such as sipping a beverage (*see also:* high tea) more than quintuples your fanciness and puts others on notice that you probably also know about things like thank-you notes and doilies.

Plumber's Crack, *noun*

Like a total eclipse, a woman cannot resist looking at it even though she knows it will scorch her retinas. It also exists in variant forms such as electrician's crack, moving man's crack, painter's crack, etc. Believed to have originated hundreds of years ago with the rise of tradesman house calls, the plumber's crack was once prized as a measure of a man's standing in the tool belt-wearing community.

These days, however, plumber's crack has fallen out of favor (especially with the women who always seem to be on the receiving end of it) and anti-crack advancements such as the extra-long T-shirt have been introduced to combat it, although with mixed success.

PMS, *acronym*

An acronym that stands for "potentially murderous situation" and is often used in reference to the exciting period of hormonal transition that a woman may experience from one to forty-seven days preceding her monthly period. As each woman's system adheres to its own slight variations in hormonal levels and cyclic schedules, the outward array of possible PMS symptoms varies and may include any of the following: 1) a mild short temper that people make a big deal about but which is actually such a *minor* thing, 2) spontaneous eruptions of explosive crying, 3) silent but ominous condemnation, and 4) sudden obsession with household chores such as gun-cleaning. A number of over-the-counter medications exist to help counteract the symptoms associated with PMS, however, research has shown that the most effective remedy is for everyone that person comes in contact with to stop being such a jackalope wang.

Pole Dancing, *noun*

A raunchy form of erotic dance in which a nude or semi-nude woman writhes around a vertical metal pole. Popularized by Eleanor Roosevelt during her tenure as First Lady of . . . [ahem] *Could you excuse us for just a moment, please?* [elevator music] *All right, we're back and we'd like to introduce Leticia, our* new *research intern.* So. Pole dancing. A popular form of erotic entertainment at strip clubs and bachelor parties, pole dancing has also made modest headway into the female commercial mainstream as both a "workout" and a "confidence-booster" (*see also:* interesting blisters).

Poncho, *noun*

What is it about a poncho? What does that question even mean? Anyway, a poncho is like a tarp for a person—you throw it on, pop your head through the hole, and most everything is covered. The poncho is one of those timeless pieces of clothing that, although it becomes trendy every so often, it never truly goes out of style, particularly if it's made from something swanky like cashmere. Bonus features of the poncho include the ease of hiding things under it (*see also:* pooch) and that it may come with pom-poms that bounce around like crazy when you run.

Pooch, *noun*

A misleadingly affectionate name for the hateful bulge that lingers just below the navel of most women. Stubborn as all hell, the pooch has been known to fight off even the most aggressive of personal trainers as well as starvation diets that would have Gandhi dialing Domino's. Not content simply to create an unsightly bulge that immediately draws the eye and generates questions about any "big news" you may be preparing to announce, the pooch may also, without provocation, suddenly inflate like an airplane's evacuation slide, leaving you immersed in regret for gorging on that extra lettuce leaf at lunch.

Poof, *noun*

A tumorous-looking mound of hair that sits on or near the crown of the head and which, while adding (sometimes significantly) to your height, also increases your wind resistance thus potentially lowering your gas mileage. Although the contemporary poof has been around for decades, it has experienced a resurgence in recent years due to its exposure on the heads of several reality television stars. The poof can be formed through vigorous and repetitive teasing of the hair while applying an industrial-strength hair adhesive or, for those who work in the vicinity of an open flame, through the insertion of a commercial hair-lifting device (*see also:* Bump-It).

Popped Collar, *noun*
An expression that refers to the practice of wearing the collar of a tennis or polo-style shirt in the vertical position so that it stands straight up around the wearer's neck (*see also:* preppy). The often-maligned popped collar appears periodically among many geographic and socioeconomic groups, and its precise social meaning varies greatly with its particular context. Although some popped-collar enthusiasts emphasize the sun-blocking benefits provided by the upturned fabric, others consider it a mark of status, and still others flip their collars up as a way of taking a stand against those who say they may not. Some popped-collar extremists are known to wear multiple polo shirts, flipping all of the collars up in a series. As colorful as this is, it looks pretty uncomfortable.

Pop Tart, *noun*
1. A term used to describe a female pop star whose outrageous attire, partying, promiscuity, or antics have eclipsed her singing career. The pop tart label is most often applied to those young women who are in the midst of this transition and about whom everyone is feigning shock that they are not turning out to be the role models everyone

thought they were. The fully loaded pop tart comes complete with an assortment of aggressively dysfunctional, publicity-hungry relatives. **2.** A delightful toaster pastry.

Pores, *noun*

The gajillions of tiny openings in your facial skin that, if inspected under magnification, will make you want to wear a pillowcase over your head the next time you leave the house. Ranging in diameter from microscopic to large enough to stub out a cigarette in, the governing principle of facial pores is the same as it is for horse jockeys: the smaller the better. Although they serve an important function for the skin that's too boring to mention here, the bottom line is that no one wants to see them and if we have to pucker them up with facial masks (*see also:* facial mask) or spackle them into oblivion with an array of cosmetic products created solely for that purpose then, by God, we will.

Precious Flower, *noun*

Euphemism for female virginity (*see also:* virgin, hymen) as exemplified in the following sentence: "I love Derek and he's been so patient with me that last night I finally gave him my precious flower." As the genus and species of the precious flower are not specified in this expression, it is presumed that a female may select the blossom of her choice when bestowing it on a deserving recipient. Note: this term is used almost exclusively by females, as males tend to draw their virginity euphemisms more from the fruit-and-berry realm.

Pregame, *verb*

Named for the rituals that herald the beginning of an athletic competition, to pregame is to drink at home or some other nonevent location in preparation for attendance at a party or social occasion. Looked down upon by some as a practice that indicates possible alcohol dependency, many view pregaming as a helpful method of social and mental preparation, particularly for a get-together that is anticipated to be emotionally challenging for some reason. For example, a woman who is the last remaining single person in her circle might pregame for a friend's baby shower in order to withstand all the well-meaning comments she's going to get about how lucky she is still to have her "independence."

Preggers, *adjective*

Loaded with subtext, the term preggers means much more than simply "pregnant." Like its cousin "preggo," describing a woman as preggers almost always carries with it a slight sneer, a whiff of snark. The use of the preggers label hints at an unspecified unattractiveness resulting from the pregnancy, and it most definitely insinuates bloating. These two terms would likely be reserved for women who are or have been in a position adverse to you (*see also:* stepwife, residual girlfriend, skank, frenemy) or whom you overheard at the company picnic dissing your jorts (*see also:* jorts).

Pregnancy, *noun*

1. (First pregnancy) A magical period in a woman's life during which she comes to realize just how magnificent the female body is while simultaneously processing the fact that not only does she no longer have a say in anything from her bathroom habits to her sleeping patterns, she also is spectacularly unqualified to care for an ice cream cake, much less a baby. It is also during this period that a woman's hormones, with which she may already have felt familiar, begin to gush like a broken fire hydrant, sending her on a months-long bender of mood gulleys, energy spikes, and emotional bungee jumps that would have a Zen master reaching for a pack of Marlboros. Then, as suddenly as it began, pregnancy ends and scrapbooking begins. **2.** (Subsequent pregnancies) Been there, done that.

Press-On Nails, *noun*

It sounds so simple, doesn't it? Select your fabulous fake nails at your local drug store, crack them out of the blister-pack and, using industrial adhesive (a 0.000002-ounce tube of which is included in the package), apply them right on top of your flimsy, eyesore natural nails. Suddenly (*see also:* BAM!), you've got the alluring, she-devil talons of a seventies airline stewardess, primed to be dug into the haunches of the nearest Burt Reynolds look-alike. Then, just as things are heating up between you and Burt, you experience catastrophic adhesive failure and—*shing!*—your paws are shedding plastic ovals like someone throwing doubloons into the crowd at Mardi Gras.

Prince Charming, *proper noun*

Sighted less often than a giant panda, pursued more relentlessly than the Son of Sam, Prince Charming (yes, it's capitalized) is the woman's ultimate prize in the romantic world. An accomplished shape-shifter, Prince Charming is many things to many women, but whether your version gallops up on a snowy stallion or roars up on a champagne pearl Harley-Davidson Softail, the bottom line is that he *gets you*. According to the instructional films (*see also:* chick flicks), you probably already know your Prince Charming but have simply overlooked him because he is: 1) the lovable rogue who hasn't met the right woman yet, 2) your brother's gorgeous but aloof best friend who's so besotted with you that he can't speak in your presence, or 3) a diamond-in-the-rough male friend who simply needs a manly makeover.

Proposal, *noun*
The occasion upon which one person asks another to become engaged and, eventually, married. Proposals tend to fall into one of two categories: spontaneous or obsessively planned, each of which gives the recipient a preview of the iron-clad, seemingly endless marital relationship to come. Although every proposal is a unique and individual expression of love, resignation, or desperation, there are some things to watch out for when fielding the proposals that are no doubt coming your way, especially as compatibility is a signifi-cant factor in marital success. For example, if you are a person who is uncomfortable drawing attention to yourself, then any proposal involving a Jumbotron might warrant the response, "Thanks. Can I sleep on it?"

Pubic Hair Dye, *noun*
A Pantone-tastic alternative to the Brazilian bikini wax (*see also:* Brazilian wax), this dye allows you to take your flair for decorat-ing all the way into your undies and upgrade the color of your pubic hair to a more desirable hue. Available at most beauty supply stores, pubic hair dye comes in "traditional" natural hair colors

as well as eye-popping shades such as fuchsia, lilac, and turquoise that will surely get you noticed at your next nudist barbeque. Until a skin-friendly fabric adhesive is perfected, pubic hair dye will continue to be the closest thing to having a throw pillow for your crotch.

Puff Daddy, *noun*

Term for the noticeable bulge of a woman's pubic area below the belly button. A natural contour of the female form, the puff daddy can suddenly become markedly apparent after a tummy-tuck procedure, which renders the waist smaller and flatter and inadvertently showcases the puff daddy. Naturally resistant to all forms of slimwear, the prominent bulge can pose a significant fashion challenge as it is almost impossible to camouflage. Beyond this practical difficulty, the presence of the puff daddy also flies in the face of the traditional female silhouette and, as a result, can cause confusion among those who encounter it.

Pulse Points, *noun*

The "correct" places on your body to apply perfume or other form of fragrance. The term's name is derived from the fact that areas of your skin underneath which there is a strong pulse will be warmer and therefore more effective at heating and disseminating the fragrance. Commonly known pulse points include the wrists, inner elbows, and base of the throat, but why stop there? Serious fragrance enthusiasts will also want to douse the brachial pulse (inside upper arm), dorsalis pedis pulse (top of foot), and facial pulse (on the mandible). Sexy, huh?

Puma, *noun*

Often confused with the cougar (*see also:* cougar), the puma shares certain characteristics with her more experienced counterpart, but can typically be found instead in the twenty to thirty-five age range. The puma (a.k.a the pre-cougar) struts across the sexual tundra, identifying her prey without thought to long-term commitment or even day-after phone calls (*see also:* most men in this age group). She has her own agenda and she has her act together. And she definitely has worked through her daddy issues because she is interested exclusively in younger men, the less clingy the better.

Push-Up Bra, *noun*

Another item in the girl's-best-friend file (*see also:* Spanx), the push-up bra succeeds where genetics do not, creating a voluptuous bustline on even the most modestly endowed chests. Through the applied use of physics, mechanical engineering, and even pneumatics, a well-made and properly fit push-up bra can give a woman the bosom she's always wanted while making everyone else wonder if she got implants during that week she was supposedly getting her wisdom teeth pulled. If applied to a woman who already has generously sized breasts, the push-up bra earns its keep by hoisting "the girls" to their optimal altitude, where they can be admired by all who enter their realm.

Queen Bee, *noun*

A ruthless despot, the notorious queen bee relies on gossip, subterfuge, and intimidation to forward her agenda within a circle of female friends. An effective queen bee surrounds herself with minions (*see also:* stooge) who lack the fortitude to stand up to her, but rather serve as downtrodden lackeys as they do her bidding. The queen bee's agenda often includes such goals as recruiting minions away from competing social circles, breaking up couples that include a male in whom she might be interested, and anything else that falls into the general category of being the boss of everyone.

Quickie, *noun*

1. A brief but mutually satisfying sexual encounter resulting when the demands of passion overrule the constraints of time. Known for its spontaneous nature, the quickie and its accompanying sense of urgency are no doubt responsible for humankind's continued quest for new and unusual locations in which to have sex. **2.** In lengthier, more established relationships (*see also:*

marriage), a rapid, efficient bout of intercourse that confirms the physical aspect of the relationship without interfering with the viewing of *Grey's Anatomy*.

R

Random, *adjective*

An adjective that doubles as an interjection and is used almost exclusively by a female to express mild consternation or rejection, or to comment on the unexpectedness of an event or piece of information. For example, "I just found out that, even though I'm in IT, I have to go to this sales conference down by the airport. How random is that?" And, conversely, "So he comes up to me while I'm dancing with my friends and shouts that we used to take our dogs to the same groomer. *Random!*"

Rebound, *noun*

Also known as a human landing pad, a rebound is a person with whom you have a relationship when you are still emotionally crippled from a recent breakup. After all, what better way to take your mind off your broken heart than to immerse yourself in the giddy beginnings of a brand new love? So what if he is the opposite of your type and you occasionally call him by the wrong name? He could grow to share your passion for ice hockey and you think his patio herb garden is really, really cute. Forget the naysayers! This could be the one rebound that goes the distance! (Laughing? *No*, we're not laughing. Absolutely not. *snort*)

Recessionista, *noun*
Frugal and creative, the recessionista laughs in the face of financial downturns and refuses to let a gloomy economic forecast overshadow her personal style. Abandon fashion just because you have less to spend? Embrace the notion that life must be dreary because the stock market has stumbled? "Never!" says the recessionista. Using the fierceness of the -ista suffix as a springboard (*see also:* -ista), the recessionista takes joy in teaching others how to get the most out of life while shooting the economy the bird.

Registry, *noun*
A detailed list of items at a particular store that you would like your friends and family to purchase for you. Gift registries are most often created in connection with a wedding, and the process of compiling this "wish list" can serve as the first test of a couple's decision-making dynamic as well as stamina. While providing guests with gentle guidance toward desired gifts and away from the horrid, crapful things people tend to buy when left unsupervised, the rigorous psycho-social process of registering can unearth troubling tendencies within even the most solid of couples. Seriously, who knew when you accepted that ring that you were making a lifetime commitment to a man who loves triangular dinner plates?

Remaining Friends, *noun*
Cousin to "It's Not You, It's Me," the concept of remaining friends after a breakup is a popular one, the goal of which is to contain

the emotional carnage of the separation. Most often employed in a breakup after which you are going to have to keep seeing/dealing with your ex (for example, he is a coworker or an integral member of your circle of friends), the invocation of the remaining friends clause allows you to claim the high moral ground. In effect, it officially establishes that you are willing to look past the breakup and honor the nonromantic aspects of the relationship, and if your ex is not mature enough to do the same, well, then who can blame you for not inviting him to your shipwreck-themed birthday buffet?

Rescue Call, *noun*
A prearranged phone call designed to give the receiver a plausible "out" during a potentially horrific experience such as a blind date or family holiday. First, you arrange for a trusted friend to call you at an appointed time, making certain that this time falls after having gotten a good look at your potential date/before your parents drain their second pitcher of martinis and start asking about that promotion they think you got. Then, when you receive the call, you release your inner actress and exclaim in horror at the fake news delivered by the caller (extra points for biting your knuckle or performing a classic sitcom spit-take on the people at the next table). After hanging up, make a hasty exit, taking care to stay in character until you are out of sight because although they know you are lying, they appreciate the courtesy of a sincere performance.

Residual Girlfriend, *noun*
The annoying physical and/or emotional detritus that lingers from a previous relationship. Like that gray-brown stuff that hangs on in the corner of the shower stall no matter how hard you dig at it with

your scrubby brush, the remains of previous relationships can be impossible to eradicate. As a result, you may find residual girlfriend cropping up in the form of a coffee mug, a photograph in the back of a drawer, even a personal joke that he tries his best to bring you into but which, considering it's just more residual girlfriend that has to be scrubbed away, is not funny. Seriously, *so* not funny.

Retail Endurance, *noun*
The ability to shop and/or browse for the long haul. Like the dedicated marathon runner, the retail enthusiast takes her avocation seriously and trains accordingly. After all, retail endurance is not acquired overnight as anyone who has cramped up just short of the entrance to Ann Taylor will tell you. The key to retail endurance is dedication to an intense, methodical training regimen that consistently pushes you to surpass your personal best and find that second wind to hit one more store, browse one more rack. Sure, there are times when you want to quit—to get your Panda Express to go and eat it in the car, throbbing feet up on the dash. But you don't quit, because you know that only the shopper who digs in for that last, excruciating checkout gets called up to The Show. That's right: the Mall of America.

Revirginization, *noun*
Wait, you can *do* this?!? [ahem] Revirginization is a medical procedure during which the remains of the thin membrane of skin that originally blocked the opening of the vaginal vault (*see also:* hymen) are surgically sewn back together to once again obscure this precious passageway. This procedure is often performed in an effort to give visual evidence of adherence to particular religious beliefs, however,

it remains up to the individual to provide convincing vocal evidence of said adherence.

Rhythm Method, *noun*
A broad term that includes a variety of calendar-based contraception methods, the efficacy of which is second only to crossing your fingers and toes. Developed for couples who do not want to use more "official" birth control methods, but who also would rather not have another baby (at least not *this month*), the rhythm method attempts to predict a woman's fertility based on counting the days before and after her menstrual cycle. Unfortunately, there is a significant margin for error—as well as babies—with this particular method.

Robotic Vacuum, *noun*
A popular household device that looks like a cross between a hubcap and a hovercraft and that will scare the liquid jeebus out of you if you arrive home and forget that you turned it loose in your house before you left. Like your Great Aunt Edna, the affable robotic vacuum likes to help out by picking up a few things here and there, but will always wait until you've settled into the bathroom with the latest issue of *Vanity Fair* before thumping on the door in need of guidance.

S

Saddlebags, *noun*

Saddlebags, also known as "mud flaps," are the fleshy fat pads that extend from the backs and outer sides of the thighs and are reminiscent of the leather carrying pouches hung across the backs of horses, such as those used by Pony Express riders. Although often maligned, saddlebags serve several useful, often discounted purposes. These include creating ideal conditions to attract a man who "likes a little something to hold on to," making the butt appear smaller by contrast, and eliminating the need to carry a troublesome stadium cushion when attending sporting events.

Scooter, *noun*

A short skirt with a pair of attached shorts hidden underneath. Certainly one of the sneakier outer garments on the market today (there are dozens of sneaky undergarments, of course), the scooter is cute, youthful, and, when the shizzle goes down, allows the wearer to lash out with a wicked roundhouse kick while keeping her drawers under wraps. Not to be confused with the skort (*see also:* skort), the scooter keeps its inner shorts a secret for all of its

360 degrees. Deceptively sweet, this garment means business and, when in the company of a scooter-wearing woman, it's wise to keep one's back to the wall.

Scrimmage Marriage, *noun*
Also known as the starter marriage, the scrimmage marriage is a short-term, initial marriage that most often involves a young couple and may or may not be undertaken with an air of romantic impetuousness. Increasingly common throughout the country, it is virtually a requirement in certain states (*see also:* California). Although some people look back on their scrimmage marriages with a philosophical view, grateful for the opportunity to absorb a few VLLs (valuable life lessons), others would prefer to purge their memories of the experience from their minds, along with their memories of hernia surgery and that time they made the racial profiling joke in the airport security line at JFK.

Scrunchie, *noun*
A stretchy, fabric-covered hair tie that, though extremely popular, is derided by some women as tacky. Once rarely seen outside the steamy confines of the aerobics studio, the humble scrunchie quickly morphed into new and exciting forms, including the velvet scrunchie, chiffon scrunchie, and scrunchie with dangling shiny things on it. The scrunchie then became a hairdo staple in the workplace and at special events before skyrocketing into popularity and eventually experiencing the backlash that inevitably follows popular success.

Fun*fact* If your cranium is small enough, you can use a scrunchie as a headband.

Secondary Virginity, *noun*

The practice of halting sexual activity and making a promise to oneself not to engage in intercourse again until after marriage. A different concept than revirginization (*see also:* revirginization), a surgical procedure in which the hymen is carefully reconstructed across the vaginal opening, secondary virginity instead involves the reconstruction of the "emotional hymen" in the form of a resolute conviction to abstain from sex until it can be enjoyed within the bonds of matrimony (whereupon you may eventually revisit the notion of abstention, but for entirely different reasons).

Security Clearance, *noun*

A ranking scale that measures the intimacy of a friendship by the degree of personal information divulged to that friend. For example, the receptionist at your office might have Level One security clearance, meaning that she knows your car and that you have a boyfriend, but not whether the car is paid for and how you *met* the boyfriend. Your former college roommate's Level Five clearance, however, indicates that she not only knows that you're two car payments behind, but that you're about to dump the boyfriend because of that thing he does in bed with his thumb. Note: security clearance levels are most often identical between close friends, as mutual destruction capability has proven to be an invaluable component in long-term female friendships.

Seven-Day Cleanse, *noun*
This phrase strikes terror in the heart of any woman who's used to eating, well, *food*. That's because the process of the seven-day cleanse is to whittle down the amount of food entering the body—or suddenly eliminate it altogether—and replace it with water, tea, or another beverage that is specially formulated to make you rethink whether having a hazmat site for a colon is really such a bad thing after all. Oh, sure, they tell you that by day five you don't notice how hungry you are because you're too busy enjoying the hallucinations, but in our opinion, if we're going to spend the weekend lying face-down in the driveway, we'd rather the cause be the toxins we put *in* our bodies, not the ones we're trying to flush out.

Sex, *noun*
Intimate and/or erotic interaction involving at least one other human being that falls into a variety of categories that include but are not limited to the following: 1) interaction that you want but can't get, 2) interaction that is plentiful but that you don't want, 3) interaction that you got but now wish you hadn't, 4) interaction that you withheld but would like another shot at, 5) interaction that you provided but feel in hindsight was not your best work, 6) interaction you are purported to have provided but have no memory of and therefore stringently deny.

Sexting, *noun*

A term created through the combination of "sex" and "texting," sexting is typically associated with teens and is the practice of using technology such as a cell phone or PDA to disseminate sexually explicit messages or photographs of yourself when you simply don't have time to run around and flash your boobs in person to everyone in your school. An organizational boon for today's students who are busy juggling homework, after-school activities, and household chores, sexting technology allows young women to organize and manage lists of the boys who would like to receive dirty talk/naked photographs, and making it easy for young men to keep track of classmate porn while staying current on their studies.

Shagreen, *noun*

Also known as "shark leather," shagreen is a type of leather that historically was made from horsehide, but the term currently refers to leather made from the hide of a shark or ray. Known by its distinctive pebbled texture, shagreen was once a popular material for use in covering sword hilts to ensure a nonslip grip. The term is now known by many women as an exotic material used in making a variety of accessories, particularly luxury handbags. Unlike other fragile exotic materials, however, shagreen is tougher than a Hell's Angel who just quit smoking, earning it the nickname "Kevlar-from-the-sea."

Shopper's Block, *noun*

If you've ever gone from store to store, flipping through rack after rack and browsing one display after another without the slightest spark of interest, you've experienced shopper's block. Estimated to have affected almost every female at least once in her consumer life, shopper's block can appear out of nowhere, striking down normal retail activities while instilling a rising sense of panic that you'll never be interested in buying anything again. A particularly pernicious form of shopper's block can be triggered by a specific retail task, such as the need to buy a gift for an occasion, at which point sufferers find themselves staring listlessly at a wall full of gift cards, tormented by the rapidly fading memories of their past gift-giving glories.

Shopping Jihad, *noun*

A relentless pursuit to track down and purchase a particular item, no matter what lengths or methods are required to secure it in the desired size and color. The shopping jihad can be parsed into numerous subcategories such as shoe jihad, jean jihad, etc. Once launched, the shopping jihad cannot be called off except by a store assistant manager who is authorized to offer a comparable—or better—item at deep discount.

Shoulder Pads, *noun*

Making their most recent trend appearance in the eighties, shoulder pads seemed to appear like mushrooms in virtually every woman's garment until they were finally eradicated in the mid-nineties. The era of shoulder pads reached its literal and figurative peak during the run of the vintage nighttime TV soap *Dynasty*, which portrayed its female characters clad in glittering gowns and luxurious, trapezoidal suits, all of which were stacked with enough foam in the shoulders to build a sofa bed. Aside from the oddly beefy stature created by shoulder pads, an additional downside existed in the undesirable migratory habits of "loose" pads that tended to peek out of sleeves and necklines no matter how aggressively they were anchored.

Size Doesn't Matter, *phrase*

Arguably one of the two most powerful and useful phrases in any woman's arsenal (*see also:* it happens to everyone), size doesn't matter is one of those unusual phrases that both the teller and tellee desperately want to be true. An integral part of the complex emotional bargain that underlies all male-female relationships, size doesn't matter is the corollary issue to the female quandary: does this make me look fat? As the man and woman address these two issues and reassure their partners with the most convincing fibs they can manufacture, the result is a beautiful symbiosis that has been keeping couples together since caveman times.

Skank, *noun*

A convenient, multipurpose term that includes but is not limited to the following definitions: **1.** Any woman your current partner ever dated, slept with, or was married to (besides you). **2.** Any women your past partners ever dated, slept with, or were married to (again, besides you). **3.** That chick who was flirting with your boyfriend at the work party—the one who was wearing the same cocktail dress you tried on but didn't buy because it made your butt look all tundra-ish but for some strange reason looked fantastic on her. **4.** Any other woman who looks fantastic in that dress.

Skinny Pants, *noun*

Skinny pants are those pants in the back of your closet that fit great only on the heels of having dysentery or in the aftermath of stomach flu. *Check it out,* you think as you admire your butt in the mirror, *I finally fit into my skinny pants!* Skinny pants are the yin to the fat pants yang—two sides of the same, esteem-propping wardrobe coin. There is one critical difference in the use of these two garments, however, and it must be respected at all times: it is perfectly fine to put on your fat pants when you are not feeling particularly fat, however, it is never, *never* advisable to attempt to wear your skinny pants when you are feeling even the least bit bloated or pudgy.

Skinorexia, *noun*
Unofficial name for dermatillomania—a condition that causes relentless picking at one's complexion. Afflicting nearly one-third of the population (mostly females), skinorexic behavior is often seen in women who also suffer from OCD, anxiety, and depression. Ironically, many women who have skinorexia do not have unusual problems with breakouts, but rather express other psychological stresses through behaviors that damage the skin. Similarly, although our living room carpet was perfectly clean already, we once went on such a vacuumorexia rampage while waiting to hear about a work promotion that in one spot under the coffee table, you can see all the way down to the padding.

Skins, *noun*
Short for exotic animal skins (faux, of course), the wearing of skins—or skin-print material—is a definite "look." Not sure if the tiger, leopard, zebra, cheetah, or other exotic-animal motif is right for you? This question is worth careful consideration because the rule of thumb with skins—just as with plutonium—is that a little goes a *long* way. Many skins neophytes get their feet wet with, say, a

leopard print belt or small zebra clutch to build up tolerance before moving on to entire blouses and, eventually, complete outfits. Others, however, leap right in with a giraffe-print jumpsuit and, whereas some women's systems can tolerate this level of fashion shock, others make the newbie mistake of attempting a full-on Rudyard Kipling pile-on, resulting in a style stampede that may require a tranquilizer dart.

Skort, *noun*

Perfect for the woman whose lifestyle includes a lot of cartwheeling, the skort (a portmanteau of "skirt" and "shorts") melds the femininity of the skirt with the modesty of shorts. Often erroneously confused with culottes (*see also:* culottes), the skort appears to be a skirt in the front (due to a clever little fabric flap) but reveals its essential shorts-ness from behind. The skort is typically short (often very short) and is designed for sporty activities such as tennis and hiking. Due to its flap front and nonflap back, the skort has been referred to as "the reverse mullet of women's sportswear."

Skunk Stripe, *noun*

Slang term for the line of dark hair that appears in your part when your artificially blonde hair color grows out and your darker, natural hair color becomes visible. It is worth noting that, decades ago, women would go to great lengths to hide the fact that they colored their hair. These days, however, the visible skunk stripe has become a style point all its own, with some celebrities even requesting that their stylists intentionally produce the effect. This development has spurred hope among women that one day soon other formerly scorned characteristics will be embraced by popular culture and that fashion's runways will be filled with models showing off their muffin-top implants and artificial chin hairs.

Slumber Party, *noun*

A female rite of passage, the slumber party, if done correctly, is so fun that you literally pee your pants with glee. Although individual practices may vary, the slumber parties of your youth that generate the happiest memories likely adhered for the most part to this classic formula: several pallets of junk food + awesome movies + sleeping bags + best girlfriends + Ouija board + gossip + spilled secrets + crank calls + shifting alliances + favorite songs + hair braiding + a long overdue falling out + more gossip + a rapprochement + totally staying up *all night!* = Best. Slumber. Party. Ever.

Smally, *noun*

An insignificant sexual encounter or interlude, as described by either gender. The smally is the fender-bender of the sexual thoroughfare, as in, "Yes, we bumped into each other but no one was hurt and then we both went on our way, leaving only slight impressions in one another." Not to be confused with the one night stand (*see also:* one night stand), the smally is the ONS's blander, forgettable sibling—the one that causes you to wonder in the middle of having sex whether your time would have been better spent sitting on your sofa and eating kettle corn while watching that bass fishing show.

Smize, *verb*

A portmanteau coined by supermodel Tyra Banks, to smize is to "smile with one's eyes." Before you scoff at this concept, you should know that for decades, psychologists have differentiated sincere smiles from insincere ones based upon the presence of crinkling around the eyes. (The crinkly ones are sincere, by the way. However, if you're getting the uncomfortable feeling that your mom doesn't like you anymore, you might want to check for Botox-induced interference.) Although smizing conjures a pleasant notion, it also raises the specter of other terms that combine body functions, such as "sprooty" (to spread one's booty) and "weavage" (to wink one's cleavage).

Smoky Eyes, *noun*

A term used to describe a style of makeup application that yields a sexy smoldering effect around the eyes that is highly prized by some women. Relying chiefly on shades of black and brown, smoky eyes comprise a dramatic look that is most fitting for evening as opposed to, say, your niece's birthday party at Chuck E. Cheese. As any makeup artist will tell you, the key to successfully creating smoky eyes is to know when to stop, as one brushstroke too many can make the difference between looking like a sultry vixen on the prowl and looking like you just removed the hood of your Batman costume.

Sorority, *noun*

Derived from the Latin word *soror* meaning sister, a sorority is an all-female organization found most often adjacent to and affiliated with a college or university. Like any social organization, sororities have vehement detractors as well as supporters. For every young woman in the so-called "Greek system" who credits her thriving collegiate social life with her sorority standing, there's another who finds the spontaneous bursts of clapping and singing disorienting and detrimental to her study habits. For those outside the system, the veil of secrecy that shrouds much of the sorority's activities feels exclusionary, but they typically console themselves by getting edgy haircuts, firing up their popcorn air-poppers, and complaining loudly in the dorm lounge about the STUPID CLUB THAT THEY WOULDN'T JOIN EVEN IF THEY WERE BEGGED.

Spa, *noun*

A terrifying facility where you are forced to slip into a freshly laundered robe then herded into a waiting area where you must lounge and read magazines containing articles with titles like "Three Smooth Steps to Relaxing into Your Calmer, Mellower Life of Balance" while sipping a cup of water that mysteriously has slices of fresh cucumber floating in it. Soon, a professional backrub-giver arrives and escorts you into a spotless chamber where rainforest sounds dribble from the ceiling and an aromatherapy candle flickers on the stone countertop. Thirty/sixty/ninety minutes later, you emerge from this room having been thoroughly lubed, kneaded, and unkinked, and are then led to any number of whirlpools and saunas where you are compelled to undergo further involuntary relaxation processing. Oh, please, don't make us go to the spa. *Please.*

Spackle, *noun*

A slang term for foundation makeup that has been applied so thickly that it looks like spackle has been smeared onto the face. Although there certainly are times when the face staring back at you from the bathroom mirror is not the one you would have chosen for yourself and the desire to "erase" it and draw a new face on top of it can be overwhelming, this urge must nevertheless be resisted. As advanced as modern cosmetics are, no product is currently available that can completely obscure your existing face. Any attempt to do so by repeatedly troweling on foundation will be counterproductive and result not in appreciative glances but in fascinated stares.

Spanx, *noun*
Friend to women everywhere, Spanx are like the sister you never had—the one who would lend you her favorite jeans, keep all your secrets, and refer to you as the pretty one. Documented antidote to the super burrito, Spanx work tirelessly to conquer and contain any bulge, jiggle, or pooch they encounter, discreetly compressing any and all excess "you" into a dense, pressurized unit. Spanx have released the modern woman from the stigma of relying on the out-dated underthings of previous generations of females (*see also:* foundation garment, girdle) while also pushing the boundaries of just how long a grown woman can go without taking a deep breath.

Speculum, *noun*
Known for its resemblance to a platypus's beak (a really *mean* platypus, to be clear), a speculum is the metal spreading device used by a gynecologist to peer into a woman's vagina. Known unofficially as "salad tongs" or "spoons of discomfort," the speculum, along with the intriguing ratcheting sound it makes, is an integral part of the rich sensory experience known as the annual exam. Note: contrary to popular belief, the speculum is not, in fact, stored in the refrigerator.

Spider Veins, *noun*
Insidious little wiggly lines that can appear anywhere on the legs, instantly adding at least a decade to your age while causing you

to seriously consider sleeping upside down like a bat to keep them from spreading. Available in either a reddish or bluish cast, spider veins are the precursor to the dreaded varicose veins, which, if left untreated, can turn your legs into a relief map of the Mississippi River and its tributaries.

Spinster, *noun*
Synonymous with old maid but slightly less derogatory, this term describes a woman who has reached an age at which women are expected to be married, and who as yet is not. Inherent in the word is the notion that the spinster has been "passed by" or in some sense left unchosen, kind of like being picked last for dodgeball, except it's not dodgeball . . . it's romanceball. Thanks to the evolving role of women and their stature in society, however, this word does not have much relevance in today's world. Instead, the word most likely applied these days to a grown single woman of independent means would be "boss."

Split Ends, *noun*
A hair dysfunction that occurs when the ends of your hair peel up from the bottom into two or more sections like string cheese. The only remedies for split ends are trimming them off or upgrading your genetic blueprint to prevent ever getting them in the first place. (Note: the latter remedy is not yet available to the general public.) You definitely knew a girl in school who spent her time finding and peeling her split ends. It grossed everyone out. She's looking for you on Facebook right now.

Sports Bra, *noun*

A highly engineered athletic brassiere designed specifically for the purpose of arresting the bustline during physical activity. As anti-jostling technology and bounce-reduction materials become more advanced, the sports bra continues to evolve in design, both structurally and aesthetically. Regardless of these advancements, however, two aspects of the sports bra remain constant: 1) the sports bra molds your breasts into a single, pressurized unit (*see also:* uniboob), and 2) the sports bra is virtually impossible to take off without smearing your lip gloss into your eyebrows.

Spray Tan, *noun*

This term most often refers to a professionally applied fake tan (*see also:* fake bake), which can be received either in an automated booth or from an airbrush artist. Although the booth method offers the benefit of privacy during the application process, a custom coating from an airbrush artist spares the tannee from feeling like she is on the losing end of an intense paintball fight that happens to be occurring in a coat closet.

Statement Jewelry, *noun*

This category of jewelry is designed to grab attention with bold design, unexpected color, and/or big-ass size. The statement necklace, for instance, is the undisputed ruler of the outfit, refusing to let the eye be drawn away from its vibrant tones, structurally complex assembly, and, often, sheer bulk. Similarly, the statement ring, with its dramatic composition and manhole-cover dimensions, pulls the eye to the hand and keeps it there. Available at all price points, this type of jewelry is the perfect accessory for the woman who, regardless of whether she knows exactly what statement she's making, wants it to come through loud and clear.

Stepwife, *noun*

Life is complicated, human relationships doubly so. Coining simple names for complicated situations goes a little ways toward making daily life more manageable. Thus, the term stepwife was born as a handle for both the ex-wife of your current husband and/or the "new" wife of your ex-husband (*see also:* wasband). Gone are messy labels like "the woman with the close-set eyes whom Daddy married after he deserted us," replaced by the streamlined stepwife, which is economical while retaining a satisfying tinge of Disney animated villainess.

Stirrups, *noun*

Not to be confused with the foot holders that hang by leather straps from a horse's saddle, these stirrups can be found at the end of your ob/gyn's exam table (*see also:* gynie). Sticking out from the corners of the table like the arms of a robot in a hurry, gynecological stirrups are designed to cradle your heels while holding your legs apart during an exam or other procedure involving your lady parts. Thoughtful doctors add an extra layer of padding by slipping oven mitts onto the stirrups, the comfort of which frees patients from the distraction of the cold metal and allows them instead to concentrate on worrying about their personal hygiene.

Stooge, *noun*

A female who lacks an independent spirit and serves as a supplicant to someone with a stronger sense of self, most often a queen bee (*see also:* queen bee). The stooge is the worker bee of the female social hive, dutifully going about her assigned tasks as another's henchwoman without complaint, never taking advantage of the fact that she could release herself from her servitude simply by telling the queen bee to cram it. Occasionally, however, a stooge will break loose from her typical persona and revolt, and when that happens . . . *heads up.*

Strapless Bra, *noun*
Second only to the push-up bra in the category of outstanding achievements in gravity-defying engineering, the strapless bra is a marvel of modern brassiere technology . . . when it works, that is. Whittled down from the old-fashioned corset, which relied on support from the entire torso to lift and showcase the bust, the modern strapless bra seeks to be sleek and minimal while providing the same support as its predecessor through the use of lung-collapsing pressure, nonslip treads, and rigid superstructure. In most cases, however, the only innovation that can keep the strapless bra from converting into an awkward belt at the worst possible moment is, well, straps.

Strap-on, *noun*
Who says you can't have the best of both worlds? For the woman who wants access to a male "situation" without having to argue over the remote, there's the strap-on, also known as a dildo harness, which allows a woman to wield male genitalia whenever she feels like it. Available in a mind-boggling array of configurations, colors, shapes, and materials, sophisticated strap-ons also have mechanical abilities that simply cannot be replicated in a traditional, analog

penis. Whether you seek the thrill of expanding your sexual prowess or simply want to cuddle without the pressure of having to make small talk, it is a statistical certainty that there is an ideal strap-on out there for you.

Stripper Shoes, *noun*

A very specific category of women's footwear favored by exotic dancers and porn actresses. Much like the decorative (and often rotating) platforms seen at auto shows and on game shows, stripper shoes are designed to catch the eye and showcase the wares. Noteworthy characteristics of these shoes include: 1) towering platforms (front and rear) or a front platform/rear stiletto combination, 2) construction from an unusual material such as Lucite, rubber, or clear plastic, 3) dramatic ornamentation in the form of charms, glitter, neon color, or animal stripe, and 4) a design that allows for quick and easy removal. Due to the extreme height of many of these shoes, it is fortuitous that most of the women who wear them have a pole (metal or otherwise) to hang on to for balance.

Sugar Daddy, *noun*

This slang term describes a man who is well-to-do and who makes a practice of financially compensating younger, attractive women for their romantic and/or sexual attentions. Not to be confused with the strictly commercial transactions that would be conducted with a prostitute, the sugar daddy models his interactions on traditional relationships, but seeks to "make up for" the discrepancies in age and physical attractiveness by providing lavish gifts of merchandise and currency to the younger woman. The continued presence of the sugar daddy relationship in modern society provides evidence that it is possible to buy a woman diamond jewelry so brilliant that it actually blinds her.

Sweater Shaver, *noun*

Okay, this thing is just plain cool. Have you seen one? It's like this little tiny airplane engine with a propeller on the front, only the propeller is super sharp like razors and it's behind a little protective screen so you don't accidentally shave your thumb down to a stump or something. Anyway, you run it across the part of your sweater that has those bothersome little fuzz balls on it (you know, the ones that appear where your arms rub against the sides of your boobs) and *brzzt* they're gone! Just like that! Also, we probably don't need to say this, but it's not a good idea to use your sweater shaver to trim your bikini line. Trust us on this.

T

Tacky, *adjective*

One of the most commanding words of all time for expressing disdain. Unlike "lame," "gross," and other comparable disparaging comments, tacky carries with it a distinctly feminine shade of condemnation that's virtually impossible to trump. Oh, sure, someone can tell you that your psychedelic caftan is butt-ugly, but just watch her crumble when you fire back that her metallic windbreaker is *tacky*. That's right, you said it. Although some sources classify the word tacky as "retro," studies have shown that the word has retained its potency through the decades.

Tampon, *noun*

One of the workhorses of Team Feminine Protection, the tampon is a small, compressed tube of super-absorbent stuff (Cotton? Rayon? Moon rocks?) that slips into the vagina and heroically holds back the flow of your monthly period (*see also:* Festival of Menses, Aunt Flo), effectively serving as the only barrier between you and social ruin. Although the basic function of the tampon remains the same across the board, the delivery method can vary from an organic applicator (a.k.a. your finger) to a compostable cardboard tube to a slick plastic applicator reminiscent of that glossy container they used when they fired Mr. Spock's body out into space in *Star Trek II: The Wrath of Khan*.

Fun*fact* Playful by nature, tampons love to leap out of your purse when you least expect it, especially when you are trying to find your wallet and pay the gorgeous actor/cashier for your soy latte.

Tankini, *noun*
A brilliant hybrid of the bikini (*see also:* bikini) and the tank top, the tankini serves as bikini with safety rails, or "training bikini" for women who are not quite comfortable with the barer look of the skimpier two-piece. Thanks to an ingenious flap of fabric that hangs from the swimsuit top and obscures most of the midsection, the tankini wearer can relax, knowing that if she forgets for one nanosecond to suck in her tummy or if she decides she simply can't resist the chili-cheese fries on the pool's snack bar menu, no one will ever know. Note: this style of swimsuit must be chosen with extreme care, as even the slightest miscalculation in sizing or design will cause an immediate shift in the minds of observers from tankini to maternity.

Tanorexic, *noun*
Combining the ideas of suntanning and anorexia, the term tanorexic refers to a person—most typically a light-skinned woman—who has gone to extreme lengths to obtain an alarmingly dark or

unnatural-looking tan, either through obsessive sunbathing or ritualistic over-application of self-tanning products or processes (*see also:*
fake bake). Tanorexics often sport an orangey, otherworldly glow
that makes both pets and other humans uneasy. In severe instances,
tanorexics' obsession renders them unable to accurately assess
their current skin tone, resulting in further suntanning or fake tan
application.

Tease, *noun*
Shorthand for more colorful terms such as "prick-tease," this is a
label often applied to a woman with whom a man has had little to
no success, sexually speaking. Well, of course she's just a tease, right?
After all, what woman wouldn't swoon for a fellow who not only
compliments her on her "awesome rack," but goes to the trouble of
asking the waiter for a second opinion? And who could possibly keep
her panties on around a fellow who eschews the term "lovemaking"
or even "sex" in favor of the phrase "put out"? Geez, he paid for
more than half of dinner—what do you broads want from a guy,
anyway?

Thank You Notes, *noun*
No one likes writing them, it's true. In fact, it's a safe bet that no one
actually "likes" receiving them either, right? Next to a mattress ad,
thank you notes may be the most boring mail you receive. Where's
the news? Where's the intrigue?

Dear Aunt Mabel, thanks again for the bitchin' toe socks.

Who needs it? And yet, there's something civilized, something *genteel* about the notion of putting pen to paper and actually forming letters with digits other than your thumbs. Gratitude in a nondigitized format? It's charmingly old-school. Wait, it's more than that. It's *analog*.

The Girls, *noun*
An affectionate nickname for breasts, most often used by women, particularly in a fashion context, as in, "That top does a much better job than the other one of showing off the girls." An appealing update to the stern "bust," referring to your breasts as "the girls" gives the comforting impression that you're not facing the fashion fates alone, but rather as part of a spunky team that includes two fun-loving companions who are always at your side (or, with the proper foundation garment, out in front of you).

The Rachel, *noun*
One of the most iconic hairstyles of the nineties, the Rachel launched a zillion layers as women stampeded to their hairdressers and demanded the cut that Jennifer Aniston sported for a portion of time on the TV sitcom *Friends*. (No, not when it was all ironed and pin-straight—that was later in the show. *Hello?!?* This was during the *first* season.) Named for her character Rachel, the bouncy, squared-off cut remains popular to this day, although Ms. Aniston remains an outspoken critic of it, calling it "ugly," which just goes to show that we never know when we look good.

The Sponge, *noun*
A contraceptive device, the sponge works to prevent pregnancy in three ways. First, the sponge itself (once moistened) becomes a dense

physical barrier that embraces the cervix like one of those stopper things that you put on top of a champagne bottle to keep the fizz in. Second, the sponge contains a spermicide that, upon contact with water, foams up like dishwashing soap, creating a sudsy trail of doom for any sperm foolish enough to cannonball into its tide. Last, any woman who has spent forty minutes performing a Cirque du Soleil–style contortionist act trying to grasp the little loop to remove the sponge will be inclined to be so hostile that she will be completely out of danger of any type of conception other than immaculate for at least a week.

Thong, *noun*
An ingenious yet potentially troublesome stealth panty, the back panel of which is designed to nestle between the bun cheeks like a garter snake between two cantaloupes. Also known as a T-back, whale tail, and the great divide, the thong is prized by most for its ability to eliminate panty lines. Others, however, remain wary of the thong due to its tendency to grind on your coccyx like a cheese grater all the livelong day (*see also*: thong burn). Note: due to the thong's inherent lack of real estate, it is recommended that you pair it with a pantiliner that has special adhesive flaps (*see also*: wings) or risk discovering the liner lodged between your shoulder blades at an inopportune moment.

Thong Burn, *noun*
An uncomfortable, raw sensation resulting from the repetitive rubbing of thong underwear against your coccyx. (No, that's not a dirty word. You can look it up.) Thong burn has been compared to sitting sideways in a swing for hours on end. A swing that happens

to be made of rope. Thong burn sufferers can be recognized by their tendency to work standing up at their desks while holding one leg out at a right angle and emitting a low moan. Also, they throw stuff.

TMI, *abbreviation*

An abbreviation for "too much information." This is a concept that we find puzzling because, frankly, we want to know it *all*. Your boyfriend's twisted bedroom practice? Bring it. Your mother-in-law left *what* in your bathroom? Tell us more! Since your liposuction procedure, your butt-cheeks are oddly asymmetrical? Let's have a look at 'em. Equipped with a powerful combination of resilience and nosiness, we are prepared to receive any information you care to share. Well, *almost* any. Your doctor says you need hemorrhoid surgery and they're going to do *what*? Okay, *ew*. TMI!

Toe Ring, *noun*

The toe ring is one of those pieces of jewelry that, when glimpsed on another woman, makes you question your life choices. There you are, waiting in line for your lunch salad in the food court before trudging back to the office to eat at your desk, and you notice the sandals of the woman in line ahead of you. There, winking sassily from the second little piggy, is a tiny gold ring with a diamond chip. This is a woman who without hesitation peels off her bikini top on a French beach, whose main mode of transportation is perched on the back of a motorcycle while clutching the six-pack of the man piloting it. You look down and study your sensible pumps. Stupid lunch salad.

Tomboy, *noun*

A term that describes a female who does not adhere to behaviors that are generally accepted as being stereotypically "female." In the classic sense, the image of the tomboy is that of a young girl who, rather than wearing a dress and sitting demurely under a tree, is instead wearing cutoffs and swinging from limb to limb of said tree. Note: many supermodels claim to have been tomboys in their youth and to have had no awareness of or interest in their beauty and other physical attributes. No one is buying this.

Topiary, *noun*

Not to be confused with full-scale Edward Scissorhands hedge-trimming, this is a fancy-sounding word for the practice of shaping your "hair down there" into various patterns, designs, and degrees of hairlessness. As new waxing fads and preferences continue to come into vogue, the possibilities for personal expression are just as numerous in your pants as they are on top of your head. Whether you opt for the utilitarian landing strip or the sexy/savage Mohawk/fauxhawk, your topiary style statement is sure to turn heads.

Train Case, *noun*

Although the train case has become a throwback in the era of lightweight, soft-sided luggage, there was a time when every woman of sophistication carried one of these when traveling—a smallish, hard-sided case with a handle on top that was never checked with the other trunks but rather carried in one's hand. It served as the armored version of the handbag, toting those essentially female items that were necessities when away from home. As such, a man would be as enthused about looking inside a woman's train case as he would be at the prospect of rooting around in his own intestines.

Training Bra, *noun*
It's a very old joke that asks the question: "Training them for *what?*" Some training is going on, however, when a young woman straps on her very first bra, regardless of its size. It is *she* who is being trained for the lifetime of tugging, snapping, adjusting, and repositioning that lies ahead of her once she becomes a brassiere-carrying member of society. Gone are those carefree days of youth when the only thing between you and the other kids on the playground was a Wiggles T-shirt. Whether you know it yet or not, you have embarked on a quest for that Holy Grail of clothing items: The Bra That Fits You Perfectly.

Tramp Stamp, *noun*
An often elaborate tattoo on a woman's body that is situated at the base of the back just above the buttocks. Those who possess these tattoos tend to select clothing that showcases them, such as low-rise jeans and cropped tops, thus inciting interest from men and envy from other women. It's believed that this envy led to the disparaging association of the word "tramp," because no one has ever seen an actual hobo with one of these tattoos.

Trendster/Trendwreck, *noun*
It's a fine line between the trendster (the woman who manages to surf the wave of *au courant* styles while making them uniquely her own) and the trendwreck (the woman who instead get picked up by that wave and pounded facedown into the sand along with her

fedora and her Ed Hardy T-shirt). A woman needs only to go one gladiator sandal too far to cross into trendwreck territory, where the fashion police (*see also:* fashion police) stand ready to issue a beatdown to those who ignore the rule of fashion gestalt: when it comes to trends, the whole is even tackier than the sum of its parts, especially *those* parts.

Trophy Wife, *noun*
Usually the second, sometimes the third or fourth, but *never* the first wife of a man who is typically over forty-five, successful, and accustomed to the upkeep required on luxury acquisitions. Not to be confused with simply a wife other than the first, the designation of trophy wife most often signifies that several factors are present in the relationship, including the fact that the trophy wife is significantly younger as well as more attractive than the husband. In this way, the trophy wife serves as visible evidence of the husband's need to deny his mortality while at the same time showcasing his impressive check-writing ability.

Trout Pout, *noun*
The unfortunate result of overzealous lip plumping procedures that leaves your mouth looking like a talking bicycle inner tube. A number of methods of lip enhancement are currently available, and although the effects of some can be counted on to wear off within a few months, others are permanent and require surgery for reversal. Regardless of the procedure selected, lip enhancement must be performed with extreme finesse as it takes only a miniscule miscalculation to reveal one's inner fish. Though often mocked, the trout pout is also considered a mark of affluence within certain social strata.

Tunic, *noun*

Part camouflage (*see also:* butt protector), part retro-chic silhouette, the wearing of a tunic, if it's properly embellished and appliquéd, can suggest that you often spend weekends in Monaco with a Greek shipping tycoon. Or, if that's a tad out of reach, the tunic can at least believably land you in the Poconos with a junior partner of an insurance brokerage. A timeless piece in any girl's wardrobe, the inscrutable tunic keeps people guessing by sending the dual messages, "Look how elegant I am in my tunic and white slacks," and, "You know, in a pinch, I could get away without wearing any pants at all."

Turkey Neck, *noun*

The dreaded slack skin or "waddle" under the chin and along the front of the neck that can appear either genetically or as a result of aging. Notoriously resistant to topical creams and scrubs, it is widely believed that the only lasting method for eradication of the turkey neck is a surgical neck lift.

> **Fun***fact* The turkey neck, though despised by its owner, has the unusual ability, especially evident at a party or other social event, to catch the available light and hold it with a prismatic effect that bystanders find mesmerizing.

Twi-hard, *noun*

A combination of twilight and die-hard, this is the term that self-described fanatical fans of the *Twilight* series apply to themselves. Known for their (literally) undying allegiance to the hugely popular teen vampire books and movies, the Twi-hards can be recognized by their typical uniform of jeans, hoodies, UGG boots (*see also:* UGG boots), and a T-shirt that advertises the wearer's allegiance to their vampire "team" of choice. Contrary to some expectations, the aforementioned hoodies may contain not only teenaged girls but also their mothers, who have become entranced by the world of *Twilight* as well, many of whom find themselves staring at their mates and wondering why they couldn't have hooked up with a nice vampire who remembers to rinse out the tub after a bubble bath.

Twi-tard, *noun*

Derogatory label given to enthusiasts of the *Twilight* series by those who are not, shall we say, fans of the vampire stories. As every special interest group has its detractors, it is not surprising that the self-proclaimed superfan Twi-hards (*see also:* Twi-hards) would have their haters, ready to poke fun at their "Team Edward" T-shirts and "Yes, I'm a Twilight Mom" license plate rims. The Twi-hard/Twi-tard conflict is just the latest entry, however, in the centuries old history of literary grudge matches, which notably include the so-called "Yawn with the Wind" agitators in 1939 and, in the early 1600s, the rabble-rousers who would cluster in front of London's Globe Theatre wearing T-shirts that read "Romeo and What's-Her-Face."

Two-Piece, *noun*

Short for "two-piece swimsuit," the two-piece category of swimwear encompasses everything from the skimpiest of bikinis (*see also:* bikini) to the most voluminous, skirted, pleated suit that happens to come in two parts. The difference between a one-piece and a two-piece is a significant one and carries considerable meaning in a woman's swimsuit-shopping process. For the woman who wants to wear a two-piece but is comfortable with a little more coverage, this category serves an important function by expanding the definition of the two-piece swimsuit beyond that of the teeny bikini to include everything from the tankini to a turtleneck and jeans.

T-Zone, *noun*
The troublesome, T-shaped area on many women's faces that insists on being oily while the rest of the face remains steadfastly arid. No doubt coined by someone behind a counter wearing a crisp smock, prismatic lip gloss, and a chip clip, the term T-Zone refers to your forehead (the top of the T) and the vertical stripe from your forehead down along your nose to your chin (bottom of the T). A very popular classification device used by skincare professionals to indicate appropriate cosmetic products, many find the use of the term T-Zone limiting as it does not take into account the particular challenges faced by women with oily earlobes (L-Zone), flaky jawlines (W-Zone), and, especially difficult to manage, the combination peeling noses/oily eyebrows (O-Zone).

U

UGG Boots, *noun*

Omnipresent Australian footwear made from shearling and available in a variety of styles, the most popular being a tall, clunky boot. The subject of UGG boots or "UGGs" reveals a deep division within contemporary society. At times UGGs have reached such heights of popularity that customers have been wait-listed for months to receive them, however some people believe UGG boots to be the ugliest, most unstylish things to appear on feet since corns. It is suspected, however, that even the most vocal public detractors keep UGGs secretly stashed in the backs of their closets to wear around their houses on weekends.

Underboob, *noun*

Known as the new frontier of cleavage, the underboob is the seam where the underside of your breast meets your chest or, in some cases, your tummy. Certain conditions must be met before the notoriously shy underboob will make an appearance. First, you must not be wearing a bra. Second, your dress or top must be strategically sliced open to reveal your midsection or must have armholes that hang down to your kneecaps.

Underwire, *noun*

The underwire bra is the Clint Eastwood of brassieres. It's not flashy, it doesn't shout, and it doesn't feel the need to explain itself to you, punk. After all, you both know why it's there: you need some extra support and you're sick and tired of being let down again and again by flimsy elastic. Well, aren't you? Now that you've experienced it, you kind of like the feeling of security that comes from having that underwire around. Sure, it's tough, but so's the job. After all, just think of everything that's riding on it.

Uniboob, *noun*

A dense yet aerodynamic mound formed on a woman's chest when her breasts are mashed together into a single unit by the confines of a sports bra. Like the bow of a Lycra-sheathed ship, the uniboob slices through any atmosphere it encounters, remaining aloft in even the most inclement weather and serving as a guidepost to fellow athletes in the gym or on the jogging path. The uniboob can also be a convenient, secure place to stash your ID and keys during Zumba class.

Unibrow, *noun*

The fetching, caterpillar-like trail of hair that can extend horizontally across one's forehead when no separation exists between one's eyebrows (of which there are typically two). The unibrow presents a considerable challenge for women—particularly those with very dark hair—who wish to divide, reshape, and generally take command of their naturally robust brow, as the plucking and waxing required to take and hold that beachhead can feel almost constant. On the other hand, there are women who reject this kind of cosmetic pruning and instead embrace the rugged naturalism of the unibrow, its linear gloss shining from the supraorbital torus like a beacon.

Unibutt, *noun*

A solid, asexual mass created when one's bun cheeks are tightly compressed against one another as a result of the application of extremely binding tights, ski pants, or elastic slimming devices (*see also:* Spanx). Not to be confused with old lady butt (*see also:* old lady butt), the presence of unibutt is not dictated by age, nor can it be predicted by socioeconomic factors. The "uni" prefix indicates that the once-dual bun cheeks have, in effect, been welded together into a single, unyielding unit that exhibits no evidence of past separateness and which may, as such, become the object of curiosity and fascination among observers.

Unwedding, *noun*

A ceremony that marks the end of a marriage, for better or for worse. Now that divorces seem to be as common as the weddings that lay the groundwork for them, there are those who feel this important occasion should be memorialized by more than a letter from the county clerk or the heaving of your formerly beloved's golf clubs into the nearest gator-infested bayou. Enter the unwedding: a social occasion that marks the official end of the marital union.

Uterus, *noun*

An integral part of the female reproductive system, the uterus is one amazingly versatile organ. Not only is it capable of dropping you to your knees with searing, spontaneous cramps, it also manages every month to produce more gore than a zombie-flick double feature. Then, just when you think you've seen it all, you become pregnant and the fist-sized uterus switches into baby mode, nestling that precious embryo and expanding to the size of a Mini Cooper as baby's arrival date approaches. Once the child is born, the uterus begins a gradual contraction to its original, compact size, a process that can take anywhere from two weeks to twenty-five years.

V

Vaginal Rejuvenation, *noun*

Not to be confused with revirginization (*see also:* revirginization), vaginal rejuvenation refers to a number of surgical procedures aimed at correcting lifelong "design flaws" in the vagina and surrounding areas, improving the overall function and appearance of these areas, or returning the vagina and its surrounds to pre-childbirth condition. For many women, the benefits of vaginal rejuvenation surgery include relief from leakage during sneezing and laughing, a more aesthetically pleasing genital area, and enhanced sexual pleasure. Much like a home remodel, vaginal rejuvenation serves as an intimate overhaul that can make everyday life more pleasant—but hopefully this type of remodel will never spawn a reality television show.

Vajayjay, *noun*

This popular slang word for vagina (*see also:* hoo haa, lemony thicket, and VIP lounge) received widespread notice in a 2006 episode of *Grey's Anatomy* and was subsequently used by Oprah

Winfrey on her show, catapulting it into the popular vernacular. It is interesting to note the friendly, sing-song quality of vajayjay (a word that reminds us of one of those adorable Pokémon characters), which is in contrast to the often warlike pet names given by many men to their penises, such as Thor, love hammer, and Mr. Shock-and-Aw-Yeah!

Vajazzle, *verb*

A groundbreaking hybrid of crafts and erotica, this term is a combination of "vagina" or "vajayjay" and Bedazzler (the popular device used to splatter metal studs and rhinestones across T-shirts and tote bags). The process of vajazzling (*see also:* labia luster) involves the gluing of rhinestones in a decorative pattern onto the skin surrounding the, um, vajayjay. Note: in order to achieve optimum results, you must get a *thorough* bikini waxing prior to vajazzling, otherwise it will just look like someone spilled art supplies on your family room rug.

Valentine's Day, *noun*

Like New Year's Eve, the approach of Valentine's Day brings on excruciating bouts of self-reflection, and not the kind that leaves you energized and ready to face life's challenges, but which instead makes you feel demoralized and ready to cut off your poodle perm with pinking shears. Although close to a billion valentines are exchanged each year in the United States, there remains a 99 percent chance that the one *you* receive will not be the one you were hoping for. Other studies have shown that you have a 96 percent chance of being the recipient of a heart-wrenchingly sincere valentine card or (God, no) gift that will require a lengthy discussion involving phrases such as "just friends" and "like a brother to me."

Valet, *noun*
A man in a little black vest who, no matter how many times you practice that Princess Diana swivel-*then*-stand move, is going to see your underwear. Like tides and taxes, the valet crotch-shot is an inevitable aspect of your time here on earth, as is the fact that you will be tipping him for the privilege of acting like you don't know he's taking your car through the In-N-Out drive-thru while you're inside the restaurant slamming down appletinis with your girlfriends and complaining about your boss (who *is* a complete assclown, btw).

Vibrator, *noun*
An extremely popular sex toy, both for autoerotic stimulation (*see also:* masturbation) and for couples who are secure enough not to mind a little friendly technological competition. Available in a stunning selection of designs and stimulation levels, there is a vibrator out there that 1) hits you in the right spot(s), 2) uses your power source of choice (batteries or cord?), 3) is sized for your portability needs, 4) matches the décor in your bedroom, garage, etc., and 5) answers to any name you feel like screaming. Thanks to the Internet, you no longer need to slip into a seedy store wearing a wig, trench coat, and dark glasses and clutching a fistful of cash to get one. Unless, of course, that turns you on.

Virgin, *noun*

Strictly speaking, a virgin is a female who has never experienced sexual intercourse (*see also:* hymen, precious blossom). As history has marched forward, however, this meaning has expanded to include both genders as well as nonsexual activities, leading to terms such as clog-dancing virgin and Scrabble virgin. Inextricably linked with the notion of purity, the term can also be applied to inanimate objects that retain some aspect of innocence about them, such as a virgin daiquiri (unsullied by alcohol) and extra virgin olive oil (gathered from the olives' very first—and hopefully gentle—pressing).

Visor, *noun*

An intriguing form of headwear that seems to appeal to the woman who likes the notion of having something on her head but does not want to commit to an entire hat. The visor is available in two styles: one that encircles the head and one that is shaped like a horseshoe and clamps onto the front of the head where its tension grip holds it in place (*see also:* migraine). Practically synonymous with the word "sporty" and very popular with the golf and tennis set, the visor works to shade your eyes from the sun while strategically leaving the part in your hair exposed for maximum sunburn potential.

Vulva, *noun*

The official name for a woman's genitals and a surprisingly (or not so surprisingly) fun word to say. "Vulva." See? *Fun.* As words for female body parts go, this is an appealing one, unlike some others we could name (*see also:* labia). Concise and economical, vulva covers the entire female genital "situation"—the whole enchilada, as it were. As handy as this term could be, however, you hardly ever hear it used in conversation, as in, "I believe I'll purchase these crotchless panties so I can showcase my vulva."

Fun*fact* The plural of vulva is vulvae, which we happen to know has been used only once in the history of civilization, and that was by Mr. George Clooney.

W

Walk of Shame, *noun*
The illustrious and unmistakable journey home in the morning following a one night stand (*see also:* one night stand). Undertaken at least 99 percent of the time by the female, the walk of shame is most notably marked by the wearing of clothing and accessories that are atypical for the time of day such as, say, a rumpled tube dress, metallic stilettos, and iridescent body glitter at 8:00 A.M. on a Sunday. Other useful indicators when identifying the walk of shame can include raccooned mascara, the presence of an evening bag, shoes dangling from the crooks of the fingers, downcast eyes, and a hurried, purposeful gait.

Wardrobe Malfunction, *noun*
A term coined by Janet Jackson and Justin Timberlake after their Super Bowl XXXVIII halftime performance in which Justin "accidentally" revealed one of Janet's breasts, which then "accidentally" seemed to poke every viewer in the world right in the eye. In the aftermath of the furor surrounding this incident of supposedly unintentional nudity, the term wardrobe malfunction has come to be a

euphemism for flashes of nudity that are claimed to be accidental, but are, in fact, "accidental."

War Paint, *noun*
A tongue-in-cheek term that refers to a woman's makeup (*see also:* face) and alludes to the notion that she is gearing up to do battle with and/or capture a man. Associated mainly with the time period of the fifties and sixties, war paint draws a metaphor from Native American culture in which warriors would often adorn their faces with dramatic colors and patterns in order to appear fiercer to their opponents. It is unknown whether any of the Native American tribes also increased their fierceness through the use of a French twist and a smart Halston jacket.

Wasband, *noun*
Shorthand term for one's ex-husband formed from the combination of "was" and "husband" and which comes packed with loads of tasty subtext depending on its inflection. This clever term is remarkably satisfying when used in everyday conversation, especially if you lean on the "was" portion of the word, as in, "There's no way I'm picking up that call because the last thing I need right now is a conversation with the *was*band." Wasband can be considered the female version of the much less fun-to-say male expression "hex-wife."

Water Bra, *noun*
An ingenious brassiere that uses strategically placed compartments filled with water to give the impression that the wearer is much more endowed than she actually is. Although some bras of this type include compartments filled with gel rather than water, the

mechanics of these two materials are the same in that they seek to duplicate the feel, heft, and appearance of natural breasts while augmenting and expanding the profile of the wearer's natural bustline. Many women rely on the water/gel bra for figure enhancement, however, others remain wary of it, citing both the hazards of embarrassing leaks and/or spills, as well as the romantic fallout that can occur when an uninitiated partner reacts to the resounding thud with which the water bra hits the floor.

Weave, *noun*
The common abbreviation of "hair weave," this refers to the practice of attaching portions of additional hair (either synthetic or human) to an existing mane for purposes of increasing length, volume, or a desired texture. Also referred to as "getting extensions," this versatile process can be applied through a variety of sewing, weaving, gluing, and bonding methods and allows you to dramatically change your style length without a pesky "growing-out" period. Unfortunately, this hair-expanding process leaves evidence in the form of application rows or "weave tracks" that owners strive to keep hidden and that, upon caressing, may snag and spirit away such items as rings, wristwatches, and cell phones.

Wedding, *noun*
The much-ballyhooed Most Important Day of Your Life during which you can expect to experience emotional DEFCON-One roughly every forty minutes, starting with the discovery that they are jack-hammering the sidewalk surrounding the cliff-side lawn where the ceremony is to be held, continuing through the cluster of gold grapes inexplicably dangling from your bouquet, the wedding

cake's road-department orange icing, and ear-splitting feedback from the minister's microphone during the vows, and ending with the inevitable outbreak of fisticuffs between your mother and step-mother. And also you get married.

Wedding Shower, *noun*
Traditionally, an all-female gathering held in the weeks or months preceding a wedding during which the bride-to-be is toasted, given gifts, and closely observed for signs of emotional fatigue and stress-eating. For out-of-town family and friends, this is typically the first opportunity to scrutinize and rank the engagement ring as well as gather intelligence about the groom that can be referenced later should the marriage fall apart. Though a bride may receive multiple wedding showers, it is the sacred duty of the maid of honor to host one of them, the process of which will strain her relationship with the bride down to its chafed and bloody nerves.

Wet Room Treatment, *noun*
This category of spa service is performed in a special room with a floor drain, ceiling spigots, and metal table that looks more appropriate for elective surgery than for a relaxing rubdown. Typical treatments of this type include the "messier" services on the spa menu, such as body polishes and mud wraps, that require extensive rinsing. Although these services can be quite relaxing, it is recommended that you ask for a full description of the procedure before booking a wet room treatment, as it can be the opposite of relaxing when you are lying naked on a metal table to be greeted by someone wearing galoshes.

Wet Spot, *noun*

The moist residue of lovemaking that tends to accumulate in the bed in the exact location in which you wanted to sleep. The wet spot, though a recent focal point of intensely pleasurable activity, quickly becomes uniquely unappealing in its gummy, post-coital chill and sends those who encounter it scurrying for cover in the far regions of the comforter. Fallout from the wet spot, including discussions regarding responsibility for the placement thereof and complaints as to whose side of the bed it is most often created upon, can be a bone of contention (sorry) for even the most established of couples.

Whipped, *adjective*

This term refers to a man who is so besotted with his wife or girlfriend that, to the disgust of his male friends in particular, he has lost all self-respect and repeatedly allows himself to be walked on by her in one form or another. Like stomach flu, the condition of being whipped can unexpectedly strike down even the stoutest of male constitutions but, unlike a passing virus, this malady has the potential to last a lifetime if left unchecked. Although you might think women would love the power afforded to them by the whipped man, it is worth noting that even the most tyrannical wife or girlfriend will eventually tire of oppressing a partner who does not at least occasionally stand up for himself.

White Dress Shirt, Men's *noun*

Surveys have shown that there is exactly one man in the United States who does *not* think a woman wearing only a men's white dress shirt is unspeakably sexy . . . and he also hates pandas and chocolate chip cookies, so there you have it. The men's white dress shirt is a slam dunk, presenting an appealing contrast between masculine and feminine while allowing the viewer tasty peeks at the delightful form within the fabric. On a more practical level, the shirt's long tail provides the wearer with an effective butt protector (*see also:* butt protector), a critical factor in the release of female inhibitions.

(To Be) Wifed, *verb*
To be wifed is to have one's professional abilities, prestige, and other attributes of one's career diminished and/or overshadowed after leaving that job to assume primary responsibility as a wife and homemaker. In other words, a married woman whose professional accomplishments appear to be "cancelled out" when she becomes a homemaker has been wifed. Scientists are currently working to discover what it is about preparing a meal or cleaning a house that has the corollary effect of erasing an upper management title or even a Harvard MBA. It's interesting to note that the term "husbanded" has yet to come into popular use.

Wings, *noun*
1. Flippy, casual bangs popularized by Farrah Fawcett and other seventies sex symbols that never looked as cool—forget about sexy—on the rest of us. **2.** Adhesive flaps found on certain pantiliners, particularly those designed to be worn with thong underwear. The wings serve as traction for the pantiliner, wrapping around the thong's crotch strap like a koala bear hugging a eucalyptus trunk. Note: despite the presence of wings, these pantiliners, like penguins, remain flightless.

Wingwoman, *noun*

The female version of the wingman, your wingwoman has got your back and, if necessary, all of your other sides as well. Mutual and deeply committed, the wingwoman relationship is most observable in large-scale social situations such as clubbing that require complex reconnaissance and secure transmission of sensitive information. The truly beneficial wingwoman connection is built over time, during which critical information is exchanged for future use, such as food allergies, romantic weaknesses, drinking habits, data regarding past breakups, and, very importantly, accurate physical description of the other's kryptonite guy (*see also:* kryptonite guy).

Woman of a Certain Age, *noun*

The English history of this phrase can be traced back more than 250 years, yet no one knows precisely what that certain woman's age *is*. Is she somewhere between mid-thirties and mid-fifties? Or is she strictly above fifty-five? Sixty-five? Eighty-five? What gives? Everyone knows that forty is the new thirty, but these days, "a certain age" is apparently up for grabs. Whatever that number is, it seems to carry with it a whiff of expiration, bringing to mind double-edged descriptions such as "well preserved." Regardless of whether agreement is reached as to the exact age of this fetching female, it is generally acknowledged that anyone who intends to apply the aforementioned label to her would be wise to do so out of her earshot.

Wonderlust, *noun*

A broader variant of ethnic joyride (*see also:* ethnic joyride) that denotes the drive to accrue a variety of sexual experiences simply to satisfy one's curiosity. Wonderlust can occur in many forms, from the fleeting admiration of the FedEx man's rippling biceps to the focused, long-term obsession with, well, just about anyone you've never had sex with. It's worth noting that wonderlust does not have to be acted upon to qualify as such. It can simply be the wondering . . . and the lusting . . . and the potent combination thereof.

X

X-bake, *noun*

A term that describes the results of receiving sun exposure in a swimsuit that has crisscrossing straps across the back. X-bake can also be used more broadly to describe the two-toned geometric aftermath of any swimsuit that features a complex, overlapping, or otherwise bold arrangement of straps or cutouts. Although the design of the swimsuit may be chic (*see also:* chic) and fashion-forward, it can be a bummer the next time you wear a sundress to realize that you have inadvertently turned your back into something that resembles a Parcheesi board.

XOXO, *noun*

Technically, XOXO is an abbreviation that most people would agree stands for kiss-hug-kiss-hug, but how exactly did the use of these specific letters come about? The X symbol has carried the meaning of "kiss" for hundreds of years, however, there does not appear to be anything inherent in the letter's shape that conveys the concept of kissing. The O, however, could conceivably represent the circle of a person's arms. If you look through the alphabet, the capital B looks the most like a kiss with its resemblance to a pair of lips pursed for an imminent smooch. So perhaps a more graphically accurate abbreviation for the notion of kisses and hugs might be BOBO. *Wait . . .*

X-Tina, *proper noun*
As illustrated in the "Xmas" abbreviation for Christmas, the letter X has historically stood as a representation for Christ (although, interestingly, you never hear anyone walk into a bathroom and exclaim, "X Almighty! What happened in *here?*"). Capitalizing on this centuries-old trend, pop star Christina Aguilera adopted the alternate name of X-Tina, which instantly added both an edgy superhero flair and a Yule-adjacent pine scent to her image. Other female superstars who have adopted alternate identities include Beyoncé (Sasha Fierce) and Mariah Carey (Mimi), although it is unclear whether either of these names has biblical origins.

Y

You Go, Girl, *phrase*

Like fresh fruits and vegetables, catch phrases can only stay crisp for so long, and this one turned to mush ages ago. That being said, however, "You go, girl!" shows no signs of extinguishing itself in popular vernacular. On the contrary, the phrase has filtered into just about every demographic stratum to the point that it has "lapped" itself and come full circle. It's worth noting that the phrase is used in earnest across large swaths of the population, whereas within certain narrow bands, it is now used only in an ironic sense that includes a tinge of self-mockery. Regardless of how you use it, this phrase deserves props for longevity. (Wait, do people still say "props?")

You're Tall, *phrase*

All-purpose expression used by diminutive women to convince women of above-average height that, no matter how ridiculous an item of clothing is, it somehow looks great on them because of their stature. Also found in the longer "You can totally wear that—you're tall!" form, this phrase has been used to push everything from floor-length sweater vests to statement necklaces to harem pants.

Although it's difficult to say whether the speaker truly believes in the beneficial effects of height or is simply messing with her tall friend, the fact is that questionable clothing items don't look any better on a tall person—they are just visible from further away.

Your New Best Friend, *noun*

A sarcastic phrase indicating that someone's interactions with you are based on her own agenda rather than sincere friendship. When spoken in reference to a female, the implication is that the female in question is attempting to use that person to get to something or someone else. For example: "You know why she's acting like your new best friend, don't you? She wants you to introduce her to your agent." When spoken by a man, the person in question will always be another man—one who is assumed to be sexually interested in you. The male version of this question is as follows: "So, who's your new best friend?" Note: your new best friend is not to be confused with, you know, your new best friend.

Z

Zaftig, *adjective*

The most common way to define this word is with the phrase "pleasantly plump." Within the context of a contemporary culture that is obsessed with being skinny, this is a tough, tough sell. Then again, zaftig has its roots in an old, old word meaning "juicy" or "succulent." That's all good, right? Sure, and pointing out someone's impotence is really just complimenting him on his impressive flexibility. In short, although this word may carry all kinds of flattering intent, it falls into the category of a "high-risk" compliment and should be attempted only by someone with the reflexes of a ninja.

Z-snap, *noun*

A sassy little gesture that involves making the outline of a big letter "Z" in front of you while snapping your fingers in these precise spots on the letter (from the snapper's perspective): 1) top right corner, 2) bottom left corner, and 3) bottom right corner. Three snaps, that's all. Not four. Four snaps will immediately expose you as a poser wannabe and your mall and/or street cred will be rescinded indefinitely. Although the beauty of the Z-snap is that it is open to broad artistic interpretation, the two meanings that are most often attached to it are: 1) "In your *face!*" and, 2) "It's *on!*" It's worth noting that this particular gesture also goes down well with a nice "Oh, no, you *di-*in't!"

ACKNOWLEDGMENTS

I am hugely indebted to Diane Garcia and Meredith O'Hayre at Adams Media for believing that my sense of humor might appeal to people other than those over whose bedtimes I have dominion and for making the process of creating this book such a pleasure. *Thank you.* Heartfelt thanks as well to Betsy Amster for her faith in me, her invaluable guidance, and for always warning me when she's about to cuss. And, although I never say "shout out," I send a grateful shout out to Kim Dower for her savvy, her warmth and enthusiasm, and her love of the color pink.

As you move through the world you meet people whose generosity changes the way you perceive yourself and inspires you to be the kind of person who evokes that feeling in others. I count myself fortunate beyond measure to include Jackie Cantor, Scott Dikkers, Beth Kephart, and Lisa See among these people.

I am enormously grateful to Chuck Andrews, Dori Andrunas, Philip Bryan, Carmella Cornett, Don Cornett, Lisa Doctor, Elizabeth Ericson, Cheryl Farrell, Lindsay Fisher, Lindsay Lang, Lisa Rae Page Rosenberg, Jacki Schklar, Leslie Schuster, Adam Sexton, Chloe Skew, Chris and Patricia Steele, Jennifer Viney, and Melanda Woo. Many, many thanks as well to all of the readers, commenters and coconspirators who make the Internet a damn friendly—and funny—place to be.

And, to my little family—Dan, Madison, and Henry—the deepest thanks of all for your patience, your encouragement and your cheers, and for providing the most loving nest a girl could have from which to spread her wings.

Anna Lefler is an award-winning writer and humorist whose work has appeared online at McSweeney's Internet Tendency, The Big Jewel, Funny not Slutty, and My Pheme, among others. Her essays on modern motherhood have been nationally syndicated. She is the author of the comic novel *Act Busy* and recently completed her second, *Doing Time in the Garden of Happiness.*

Anna has performed standup comedy in Los Angeles clubs including the Hollywood Improv, the Comedy Store, Room 5 Lounge, and M Bar. She presented her humorous essays at Women Who Write in Los Angeles and appeared in the "Listen to Your Mother" show in the Los Angeles cast of its national program. Anna's fiction has been presented onstage by WordTheatre Los Angeles.

Anna writes a popular humor blog called *Life Just Keeps Getting Weirder* (*LifeJustKeepsGettingWeirder.blogspot.com*), where she ponders what a Jedi smells like and wonders why more men don't wear urban sport kilts. She has twice been asked to speak on the topic of comedy-writing at BlogHer, the world's largest conference for women in social media.

She lives in Santa Monica, California, with her husband, their son and daughter, and some judgmental dogs. Visit Anna at *www.annalefler.com* or follow her on Twitter: @AnnaLefler

Getting Where Women Really Belong

- Trying to lose the losers you've been dating?
- Striving to find the time to be a doting mother, dedicated employee, and still be a hot piece of you-know-what in the bedroom?
- Been in a comfortable relationship that's becoming, well, too comfortable?

Don't despair! Visit the Jane on Top blog—your new source for information (and commiseration) on all things relationships, sex, and the juggling act that is being a modern gal.